2004 PC

ONCE UPON A RHYME

IMAGINATION FOR A NEW GENERATION

Cambridgeshire Vol II
Edited by Steve Twelvetree

Young**Writers**

First published in Great Britain in 2004 by:
Young Writers
Remus House
Coltsfoot Drive
Peterborough
PE2 9JX
Telephone: 01733 890066
Website: www.youngwriters.co.uk

© *Copyright Contributors 2004*

SB ISBN 1 84460 599 0

Foreword

Young Writers was established in 1991 and has been passionately devoted to the promotion of reading and writing in children and young adults ever since. The quest continues today. Young Writers remains as committed to engendering the fostering of burgeoning poetic and literary talent as ever.

This year's Young Writers competition has proven as vibrant and dynamic as ever and we are delighted to present a showcase of the best poetry from across the UK. Each poem has been carefully selected from a wealth of *Once Upon A Rhyme* entries before ultimately being published in this, our twelfth primary school poetry series.

Once again, we have been supremely impressed by the overall high quality of the entries we have received. The imagination, energy and creativity which has gone into each young writer's entry made choosing the best poems a challenging and often difficult but ultimately hugely rewarding task - the general high standard of the work submitted amply vindicating this opportunity to bring their poetry to a larger appreciative audience.

We sincerely hope you are pleased with our final selection and that you will enjoy *Once Upon A Rhyme Cambridgeshire Vol II* for many years to come.

Contents

Eloise Ludlam (9)	24
Eve Harwin (8)	24
Ruari Clark (9)	25
Holly Gibbons (8)	25
Hannah Allan (9)	26
Jessica Cole (9)	27
Cameron Wishart (8)	28
Jessica Broomfield (9)	29
Ben Herbert (8)	30
Ryan Son (9)	31
Jack Cooper-Riddiford (7)	32
Samuel Bradshaw-Clifford (8)	33

Castle Camps CE Primary School

Cara Ainsworth (11)	34
Benjamin Messenger (11)	34
Penny Ardley (10)	35
Emily Chapman (11)	35
Jade Bester (11)	36
Angus Parks (11)	36
Natalie Haylock (10)	37
Laura Elmer (11)	37
Anna Barker (11)	38
Kirsten Goldstone (11)	38
Alice Webb (10)	39

Dogsthorpe Junior School

Natalie Lemin (11)	39
Fiona Macdonald (10)	40
Charlotte Cooper (11)	41
Melissa Wynne (11)	41
Jade Walker (11)	42
Paris Wilson (11)	42
Olivier Popple (10)	42
Sophia Curran (10)	43
Matthew Vernall (10)	43
Patrick Newton (10)	44
Jennifer Goodman (10)	44
Harriet Musson (11)	44
Giordan Gregory (10)	45
Lauren Wood (9)	46

Jannette Taylor (10)   46
Adam Pettit (9)   47
Natasha Mohan (10)   47
Patrick Holding (10)   47
Perry Saunders (9)   48
Gabrielle Albert (10)   48
Sarah Chambers (10)   49

Emneth Primary School
Robert Wells (11)   49
Emma Barker (11)   50
William Tysterman (11)   50
Craig Durrant (10)   51
Megan Bywater (11)   51
Nathan Ramm (11)   51
Genevieve Williams (11)   52
Katie Sykes (11)   52
Luke Goodall (11)   53
Hannah Drewery (11)   53
Lee Punter (11)   54
Oliver Porter (10)   54
Alastair Hardy (11)   55
Monique Harris (11)   55
Morgan Ritchie (10)   56
Lucy Downham (11)   56
Robert Elcock (11)   57
Jack Edgson (9)   57
Abigail Rose (7)   58
Rebecca Hanley (9)   58
Charlotte Ward (8)   58
Kieran Jakings (8)   59
Abigail Garrod (8)   59
Joshua Garrod (11)   59
Claire Mead (8)   60
Gemma Cooper (9)   61
Lisa Williamson (10)   61
Shanice Moyses (11)   62

Great Abington CP School
Harry Franklin (8)   62
Karina Brammah (9)   63

Evie Haugh (10)   63
Antonia Eady (8)   64
Jordan Raven (9)   65
Lucy Olivia Edgar (8)   65
Penny Malpass (9)   65
Christopher Nightingale (8)   66
Alice Merryweather (8)   67
Hannah Malpass (9)   67
Charlie Froment (8)   68
Jessica Howe (8)   68
Alex Taylor (9)   69
Robyn Hammond (8)   69
Stacy Drieu (9)   70
James Harrison (9)   70
Anna Krylander (9)   71
Rachael Cornwell (9)   71
Evie Roddom (7)   71

Holme CE Primary School
Emily Bugg (9)   72
Alexander Collins (9)   72
Molly Edwards (10)   73
Abigail Tandy (10)   73
Laura Davies (11)   74
Adam Spratley (11)   74
Gemma Custance (9)   74
Leilani Barratt (9)   75
Bethany Wilkins (11)   75
Lucy Walters (11)   76
Amelia Tillson-Smith (11)   76
Martha Cattell (11)   77
Stuart Rennie (10)   77
Philip Spriggs (10)   78

Longthorpe Primary School
Sam Dane (10)   78
Leon Hamid Ouardighi (10)   79
Trevena Bisla (9)   79
Ross Symns (10)   80
Abby Calderbank (10)   80
Monique Williams (9)   81

Rebecca Jones (10)	81
Reza Petersen (10)	82
James Lovell (9)	82
Michael Russell (10)	83
Hannah Sharman (10)	83
Charlie Ding (9)	84
Ashley Watson (10)	84
Iram Hussain (10)	85
Christina Mudge (10)	85
Lizzie Mallett (10)	86
Jennifer Chaney (10)	86
Becky Stevenson (10)	87
Ahkeel Mahmood (10)	87

Perse Preparatory School

Joshua Fenttiman (10)	88
Thomas Myers (10)	89
David Meredith (10)	90
Jonathan Butler (10)	92
Edward Noble (10)	93
Ryan Anand (9)	94
James Hopkin (10)	95
Nicholas Lander (10)	96
Nicholas Li (9)	97
Robert Lowther (10)	98
William Harris (10)	99
Howard Danner (8)	99
Christopher Littlefair (10)	100
Tom Norris (11)	101
Eddie Addo (10)	102
Alex Pak (10)	103
Thomas Reynolds (8)	104
Andrew Green (7)	104
Angus Osborn (10)	105
Max Palmer-Geaves (10)	106
Jamie Seaward (10)	107
Alasdair Stores (10)	108

St John's Church Primary School, Peterborough

Rachel Christie (10)	109
Jemma Speight (10)	109

Josh Munday & Emily Hammond (11)	110
Shayn Smith (11)	110
Nathan Brown (11)	111
Joanna Pullinger (11)	111
Andrew Stephenson (10)	112
Stephen Burn (11)	112
Emma Hume (11)	113
Marina Hansen (10)	113
Lynette Barnett (11)	113
Stuart Firth (11)	114

Swaffham Bulbeck Primary School

Connor Wormald (9)	114
Matty Garner (9)	114
Adam Judge (9)	115
Shannon Wright (8)	115
Ben Barrett (9)	115
Megan Pedersen (9)	115
Sam King (8)	116
Poppy Crossley (8)	116
Hannalise Tirrell (7)	117
Chelsea Oliver (8)	117
Ellie Crossley (8)	117
Amy Mockridge (7)	118
Shannon Manchett (9)	118
Dominic Ambrose (9)	118
Laura Foreman (8)	119
Ellen Rayner (8)	119
Joe Acklam (10)	120
Hannah Hudson (10)	120
Jessica Rayner (10)	121
Emily Rawlinson (10)	121
Jake Cronin (10)	122
Molly Preston (10)	122
Martin Lively (10)	122
Sabrina Taylor (10)	123
Aaron Smith (10)	123
Alex Garner (10)	124
Miriam Willmott (11)	124
Tilly Newbury (11)	125

Zoe Ball (10)   125
Lucy Parker (11)   125

Teversham CE Primary School
Amy Mills (8)   126
Katie Logan (7)   126
Jessica Adams (8)   127
Scarlett Diver (7)   127
Rama Lakshman (8)   128
Ashley Reid (8)   128
Laura Shephard (8)   129
Jake Brown (8)   129
Melissa Pettitt (8)   130
Abigail Bell (8)   130
Jake Bowden (8)   131

William Hildyard CE Primary School
Olivia Brown (7)   131
Katie Webb (8)   132
Daniel E Luff (10)   132
Ben Winspear (11)   133
Oliver Lansell (11)   133
Thomas Burton (10)   134
Hasnain Datoo (11)   134
Ben Windsor (11)   135
William Burton (10)   135
Rebecca Potton (8)   136
Marcus Cook (8)   136
Charlotte Hussey (7)   136
Danielle Raven (10)   137
Jake Brown (7)   137
Laura Aldington (7)   138
Leah Potton (7)   138

Woodston Primary School
Sharnee Baker (11)   139
Jordan Greer (11)   139
Hannah Hillan (11)   140
Jamie Cook (11)   140
Amy McLennan (11)   141

The Poems

Swimming, Swimming

Swimming, swimming
In the pool
Diving, diving
Off the board
Backflips
Off the side
Forward flips
Off the other side
Jumping, jumping
In cold water
Front crawl, front crawl
Is the best
Weeing, weeing
In the pool
Naughty, naughty
People.

Emily Priest (8)
Brampton Junior School

Dancing

I like dancing everywhere,
At home, everywhere.
In the garden,
In the drive,
I like dancing.

I like dancing everywhere,
In the study,
In the kitchen,
Oh no! *clatter, dong, dong.*
I think I knocked something over!

Michael Sweetenham (7)
Brampton Junior School

My Trip To Mepal

M y trip to Mepal was so much fun
E xciting on the bus when we got there everybody shouted
P layed on the playground
A ll together
L ots of games

R unning about
E arly to bed
S oon it was morning
I mpatient for the next activity
D irty washing
E nergy for the next activity
N ormal days
T rust trail
I enjoyed it
A ctually, I did enjoy it, lots
L ots of laughing.

Jacqueline Page (9)
Brampton Junior School

Being Bored At School

I'm bored, bored, bored.
I don't want to waste my day.
So please excuse me from school today.
I want to go out to play.

Now it's playtime.
I'm playing football.
Oh no! Oh no! Oh no!
I have to go back into school.

Charles Powlson (8)
Brampton Junior School

Animal Alert

If you ever met with an angry kangaroo
Don't run or scream
I'll just tell you what to do.
Stand as still as a tiger
And as thin as a bat
Don't move a muscle
Or you'll be knocked flat.

If there's ever a snake in your bed
Go running downstairs
Just don't dread.
Get a large stick
I'll give you a clue
Pick up something
Don't go hullabaloo
Put it outside
And get into bed.

Kathryn Cockrill (8)
Brampton Junior School

My Cat Sly

I have a cat
His name is Sly
And he sleeps on a mat!

We call him Sly because he is sly
He is not yours, he is my cat
He just lies about!

He is a greedy cat
He even eats on the mat!

Hayley Nicholson (8)
Brampton Junior School

Alphie, My Dog

I have a dog called Alphie
He is always very good
He always wants to play with me
Always after lunch.

We always play catch
Alphie never cares if he doesn't catch the ball
But when it is bedtime
He jumps in with me.

When it is morning
He always scratches me
But when he scratches me
It doesn't really hurt.

Rhiannon Hazle (7)
Brampton Junior School

Animals

Laughing lion
Extraordinary elephant
Wicked wallaby
Incredible iguanadon
Sizzling spiders
Fiddling flipper
Only octopus
Untidy umbrella bird
Naughty nocturnal fox
Talking tarantula
Aging animals
Interesting iguana
Nice natterjack toad.

Dan Gemmell (9)
Brampton Junior School

Mepal

M essy room for inspection. My room is definitely not going to get it.
E ating nice food but the cook was a little bit stressful
P lanning to go to bed, but Ben did not let me
A nother day of fun activities, I hope I do trampolining again
L earning new things on every activity.

R eading my book of true ghost stories
E xtra fun in rock climbing, but more fun in trampolining
S leeping was good when Ben let me sleep
I n snorkelling I saw a pike, it was cool and fun as well
D essert was delicious and so scrumptious
E xciting fun from all of the activities
N ormal stuff happing in the morning
T he trust trail was fun, you didn't know what your partner would do
I n sailing I nearly fell in. Kyle pulled the rope, the metal pole hit me
A nd raft building was fun too
L azy me, lazy me, not getting out of bed.

Jimmy Witherall (9)
Brampton Junior School

In School

I worked outside
N ext I made a card

S at somewhere new
C lassroom is different
H aving to be in a Year 3 class
O nce did maths with Year 3
O nly one person I know
L ast days, made flapjacks, *yum!*

Courtney Fain (9)
Brampton Junior School

Mepal

M aking rafts and designing them was exciting
E ating the food was yummy
P ractising a speech was really fun for room inspection
A nd exciting games finish at 8.30, my favourite was the last one
L aughing my head off was great.

R unning away from people for the last games
E xciting doing archery, especially not going on a date
S ailing with Hannah was fantastic
I thought that snorkelling was OK
D eciding what to do when I went sailing was hard
E nd of day, tired. I need sleep. Asleep by 10.30
N ew day, get up and ready. Can't wait
T idy bedroom for inspection
I was excited to go home but wanted to stay
A long day, ready to go home
L aughing on the coach, what busy days.

Brontë Dines-Allen (8)
Brampton Junior School

Dolphins

D olphins love to splash around
O ver the ocean and in the sea
L oving, gorgeous, pleasant, kind
P orpoises are closely related
H appily floundering around in the wavy sea
I am a dolphin lover
N early breaking the somersault record
S ome dolphins are special
    Just like you and me!

Zahra Hussain (8)
Brampton Junior School

Mepal

M oving in the coach
E xtremely excited
P ushing on my snorkel mask
A fter an introduction
L osing concentration in archery.

R ocking with laughter
E ating up my tea
S earching for my underpants
I n my dormitory
D iving into the freezing lake
E xtra wet, you'll see
N ever ever giving up
T rying my best
I n the rock climbing room
A ching in my chest,
L ie down in the coach, *argh!*

Thomas Wilkinson (9)
Brampton Junior School

Dogs

P utting their cute faces on you for a hug
U nder your legs telling you they want to go for a walk
P ups on the pillows
P aws paddling in the water
Y ou think your dog is going to talk.

D ragging their long hair on the ground
O ld dogs cry, cry again
G olden coats shining in the sun.

Faye Honeybun (8)
Brampton Junior School

Mepal

M r Farmer bailing out with a plastic cup
E verybody laughing, oh look, oh look, oh look
P eople, it's all Becky's fault
A ll the way back on
L and.

R uari was snoring
E verybody's having fun
S un, oh sun
I love the sun
D id it rain? Not a bit
E ven when I missed my mum
T he coach is here
I 'm going to see my mum, how great
A ll aboard onto the coach
L ook, oh look, we're back at last.

Jack Galbraith-Edge (9)
Brampton Junior School

Puppies

Long legs
Short legs

Yappy puppies
Quiet puppies

Bald puppies
Fluffy puppies

Skinny puppies
Fat puppies

Cute puppies
Sleepy puppies.

Victoria Crane (9)
Brampton Junior School

Football

Football is always fun to play,
Try not to kick me in the face,
Work together to get that goal,
Beckham's number 23,
Just get that goal in there,
When you win it's time to cheer,
Winter's always wet
Summer's lovely and warm,
First yellow card, then red,
Leeds breathtaking, always there,
Winning the Premiership,
Trying as hard as they can,
Getting a goal, supporters cheer,
Winning the games,
Running around the pitch,
As you get that goal.

Jessica Sargent (8)
Brampton Junior School

Summer School

S izzling sunshine
U nder the tree
M aking daisy chains
M ore maths
E xcited children
R unning races

S ports day is fun
C old and windy
H appy playtime
O ld friends, new friends
O nly one more day
L ovely, long holiday.

Sophie Mooney (9)
Brampton Junior School

Miss Hughes' Class

A t Miss Hughes' class it was great
B oxes and bottles and painting was amazing
C oaches arrived at 9.30 to go swimming
D ived down in the water and I did a flip
E lliot thought he saw a dragon
F ootball games are spectacular
G lue was very sticky
H andstand in the pool
I like the coach because we were bumping and laughing
J oking around in the swimming pool
K icking a ball in the swimming pool
L unchtime and it was great
M ythical creatures were fantastic
N oah chased Thomas around the pool
O h, Elliot went crazy in the swimming pool
P arachute games were extraordinary
Q uickly Elliot chased Thomas and me
R ace to the swimming pool
S wimming was tremendous
T he coach was bumpy and everybody was laughing
U nder the door we found a key
V ery much I liked swimming in the pool
W e got extra playtime
X rays I did not need
Y ou did a brilliant book of spells
Z ebras were not in Miss Hughes' class.

Noah Foster (8)
Brampton Junior School

Acrostic Poem

A t Grafham Water it was good
B ecause it was fun
C an you windsurf?
D ucks go swimming
E veryone is having fun
F un and games
G oing to bed
H aving fun in the sun
I liked the food
J umped on the beds, it is fun
K icking the football was fun
L a, la, la we sung
M y friend fell over the wall
N ow I am having fun
O utside it was fun to play
P eople were nice
Q uite cold water
R unning to Grafham was fun
S un was out it was a nice day
T he bed was comfy
U nder and over
V ery tall tower
W e had great fun at Grafham
X rays we did not have
Y ucky mud
Z zzzzzzzzzzzzz!

Alice Stewart (8)
Brampton Junior School

Mepal

M y favourite food was hot dogs
E veryone liked the activities
P eople played in the park
A nd I was terrified of snorkelling
L ovely rooms with a basin.

R eally, we should have been more quiet
E very time I went down the slide with my mouth open
S oon I started to miss my mum
I really liked trampolining, it was my favourite activity
D awn came very quickly, almost suddenly
E vening was very nice because we had hot chocolate
N early everyone believed there was a croc in the lake
T he park was fantastic, it was really fun
I didn't want to go home
A nd nearly everyone went to sleep on the coach
L isten, you can hear the children singing.

Lucy Galbraith-Edge (9)
Brampton Junior School

The Sea

Waves crashing and bashing against the hard rocks,
Boats sinking on stormy days,
The moon reflecting on the dark water at night,
Fishermen going out on their wooden boats in the morning
to catch fish,
Starfish clinging onto the bumpy rocks in the watery rock pool,
The waves sweeping up smooth stones into the deep sea,
Seagulls swooping down to the water to catch slippery fish,
Orange crabs walking along the smooth, yellow sand,
Shiny fish darting in and out of the sharp rocks,
Dolphins diving into the cold, dark water.

Isabella Read (8)
Brampton Junior School

Mepal

M aking a raft
E ating the yummy doughnuts
P addling in the boat
A rchery was fantastic. I got a bullseye
L arger raft to get it right.

R acing in the raft. We won!
E nergy was in us and we just kept on going
S eeing lots of fish when we were snorkelling
I n the night we went to bed straight away
D ormitories were small but cosy
E nough things for one day
N ature all around us there
T he best bit was capturing the flag
I n the end we went into the bus
A nd we were very sleepy
L aughing at the number of football players in the bus. We got 71.

Connor Belgrove (9)
Brampton Junior School

Dogs And Puppies

D ogs' tails waggling all day long
O f all the dogs in the world my dog won
G oing to see dogs winning sparkling prizes
S ome dogs small, some dogs large.

A ll day long we were there
N o people feeling sad, all very cheerful
D ogs all different types and colours.

P ups there as well
U p on the podium
P eople playing with dogs at home
P laying with dogs, playing with dogs
Y ou could get a dog today
S orry, *now* it is over, see you tomorrow!

Abbey Merritt (8)
Brampton Junior School

Mepal

M y room was great
E veryone ate
P eople playing games
A nd hoping we don't feel rain
L istening to the water, *splish, splosh, splash!*

R unning round in circles, I hope our raft will float
E veryone excited, we captured the flag
S norkelling was fun but we didn't see a croc
I went as high as the sky on the trampoline
D arting around in my little sail boat
E veryone went rock climbing, we climbed so high
N ight-time was hard, we couldn't get to sleep
T rust trail was tricky, we went over a swamp
I loved playing warships, I sunk all my friends
A t the end of the day, everyone was wet
L ovely coach, good ride home. Miss you Mepal. Bye-bye.

Natalie Primavera (9)
Brampton Junior School

Karate

K icking the air with our concentrating eyes
A iming at the practise fighting stuff
R acing fists and air with total concentration
A ttacking the karate bag and puff
T aking our black suits to training
E lecting two excellent people of the week.

Michael Wilson (8)
Brampton Junior School

Mepal

M epal outdoor centre
E xciting things to do
P laying on the climbing frame
A rchery was good fun, shooting arrows
L ovely hot chocolate.

R ock climbing was fun and exciting
E nergy helps you do everything
S norkelling in the warm lake seeing fish
I n a boat, sailing
D arcie liked trampolining
E nergetic games after tea
N oisy people snoring
T ubs and ropes to build a raft
I n the day Mr Farmer and Simon sang Abba songs
A ll the children were tired
L ying asleep all the way home.

Darcie Burcham-Brown (9)
Brampton Junior School

Australia

Australia is burning hot
The desert is dry and dusty
Poisonous spiders hide away underneath the cacti
Beautiful sandy beaches
Excited children running in the sea
Crashing waves knock me into the strong, strong sea.

Ben Scott-Jeffs (7)
Brampton Junior School

Mepal

M y trip to Mepal was so great
E vening activities made us stay up late
P laying in the water was so much fun
A nd eating lots of hot dogs in a bun
L unchtime is at half-past twelve.

R unning in and out of tyres
E ating some ice cream all in a team
S norkelling in the water made us all scream
I nside showers were all nice and warm
D rying myself, but not in a storm
E vening comes along so fast
N ight-time and bedtime were at half-past nine
T eachers are being funny
I thought they were being kind
A t the end of Wednesday I packed my bag
L ater on I'm back home. Let me go again!

Olivia Bicknell (8)
Brampton Junior School

Football

Football is a magnificent sport
And can teach you lots of skills,
For shooting you need plenty of power
And for tackling you need speed,
Do your skills, then score a goal,
People win and people lose,
When you play you become exhausted,
All teams have lots of water,
'Half-time!' calls the manager.
After the break the game goes on,
You score some more goals then and now,
When a team scores, the crowd goes wild!
The ball's like a light bulb flying in the air,
Ninety minutes gone, the match is over,
Every single player all going home,
Everyone tired, all going to bed.

Ellery Pullin (8)
Brampton Junior School

Football Crazy

The best sport you can do
Sometimes the underdogs come through.
Adrenalin running through the players' veins,
Arsenal, Man U, Newcastle are all tremendous teams.
Loads of pressure on the goalkeepers, defenders, midfielders
And strikers, but all are an essential part of the team.
It's an extraordinary game.

George Wooff (8)
Brampton Junior School

With Miss Hughes

A n excellent day with Miss Hughes
B usy people everywhere
C limbing, canoeing, *argh* my head hurts
D oing what we need
E xciting things to do
F un and exciting
G oing to the door
H aving lots of things
I enjoy myself
J oshua wasn't there
K it to get now
L ots of fun things to do
M ichael with me
N ot boring at all
O h dear, I'm losing my head
P eople having lots of stuff
Q uestioning
R unning, having lots of fun
S wimming pool, we had some floats
T homas was silly
U nclean me, unclean me
V ery fun, very fun
W hy did we not go to Grafham?
X ylophone we did not play
Y ou are having fun too
Z ebras weren't there.

Sean Lawson (8)
Brampton Junior School

Swimming

A week of fun is here
B ut how I miss Miss Norman and the class
C oaches arrive
D own to them we go
E lliott thinks he's seen a dragon
F irst in the swimming pool was me
G oing under hoops was difficult
H aving no goggles
I tried surfing
J ust came off worse
K icking the water
L ike a slippery fish
M ike is hogging the balls
N ow's the time to sneak up
O n him
P addling quickly
Q uick, quick, quick
R ound a corner
S lickity slick
T earing through the water
U nder hoops
V anishing under the blue
W ith a smile on my face
X ylophone playing we did not do
Y ou just can't get out of the pool
Z zzzzzzzzz, it's so tiring!

Thomas Kilkenny (8)
Brampton Junior School

Football

F antastic players shoot for glory
O pponents shiver as it just starts
O ur team are the best
T ired as they were afterwards
B etter than the rest
A ll players are the winners
L osing doesn't matter
L earning to play football

I njuries hurt a lot
S hots were smashing

G reat players
R ushing to score
E njoy football as well
A n enormous crowd
T op of the football league. England is there, the best!

Chris Parker (8)
Brampton Junior School

Mepal

M y trip to Mepal was so great
E ven activities made me stay up late
P aintballs everywhere made me trip and fall
A nd eating hot dogs in a scrummy bun
L ovely instructors helping us get it done

R aft building was so much fun
E very day was great
S o I ate and ate
I nside the
D ormitories it got quite hot, so
E veryone is inside the boiling pot
N ight-time feasts were scrummy
T rampolining was really exciting
I n and out the café
A nd saying goodbye was hard
L ong journey home.

Caitlin Kennedy (9)
Brampton Junior School

Grafham Days

A ndy was extremely silly
B eef for tea
C limbing was hard for some but I got to the top
D orm inspection on Thursday and Friday
E very evening we went to the tuck shop
F or breakfast I had Coco Pops
G rafham challenge was extremely muddy
H ard work to go up the hills on bikes
I loved to do activities with Miss Norman
J umping Miss Stirling always winning top trumps
K illing ourselves up hills on bikes
L ow ropes were very fun
M ountain biking was tiring
N ext comes Miss Norman the most beautiful of them all
O rienteering was very hard
P aul and Rob singing songs when we were about to go
Q uiet dormitories in the middle of the night
R ock climbing was really fun
S ophie was excellent at annoying Andy
T he activities were very, very fun
U niverse was noisy with us at Grafham
V isiting Grafham water centre
W alking to our letters when we did our orienteering
X -rays not needed
Y ou just can't get away from Grafham
Z ing-zing, the xylophone was not the dinner bell.

Sophie Ryder (7)
Brampton Junior School

Mepal

M y trip to Mepal was so great
E vening activities made me stay up late
P aintballs everywhere, made me trip and fall
A nd eating hot dogs in a scrummy bun
L ovely instructors helping us get it done.

R unning about playing games
E xciting playing on the trampoline
S ailing and snorkelling was so fun
I n the lake getting wet
D oing rock climbing was amazing
E ating yummy food
N ight-time feasts are scrummy
T rampolining was really exciting
I nstructors were really nice and kind
A nd saying goodbye was hard
L ong journey home.

Fariyah Aisha Parwaiz (8)
Brampton Junior School

Animals

Animals are extremely soft, some are very smooth
Some are very wrinkled
Some are big, some are small
And some are even bushy.
Some are rough, I like most animals because they are cute,
Some are speedy, some are incredibly slow,
They can be tall, they can be small,
Different colours of animals.
They are sensational at huge jumping
And they have got furry tongues,
Certain ones are wet, others are dry as a bone,
When it's hot they need lots of liquid,
Some have long necks, others have short, stumpy legs,
Some have sharp claws.
They have enormous teeth so they can munch their food.

Jonathan Wrycraft (8)
Brampton Junior School

Mepal

M e and Becky went raft building and we fell into the river
E xcited
P laying games at night
A t archery it was really fun we played this game
L earning new things

R ebecca, Fariyah, Caitlin and me were excited
E verybody was really noisy
S norkelling, we went snorkelling and I went into the river
I n our dormitories Becky was being really funny
D inner, we all had macaroni cheese
E nergy, lots was used
N oisy children in the dormitories
T he park was fun and we all played in the ball pit
I n the hall we did trampolining
A t breakfast I had scrambled egg on toast, so did Fariyah
L ucky us!

Eloise Ludlam (9)
Brampton Junior School

The Sea

Rocking waves I can see
The sun so hot on me
Different coloured rocks I see
Seaweed twisting and turning so green
The clouds of the sea so soft and calm
Sand and stones crash, bash and nash
Fish darting and gliding
Getting out of the way of the weeds.

Eve Harwin (8)
Brampton Junior School

Mepal

M rs Holland was our group leader
E arly starts for all
P eople standing everywhere
A rchery was cool
L astly, was our lovely lunch

R uari snored till he woke up
E verything was hard for us
S norkelling was too
I found it really difficult
D oing climbing was wicked
E njoying everything
N aval war games was lucky
T he cook was stressed, she shouted at everyone
I n the lake it was incredibly cold
A ching in my stomach, I'm exhausted
L ie down for bed!

Ruari Clark (9)
Brampton Junior School

Popstars

P op songs rocking in my room
O bviously I will boogie to the tune
P eople watching rockets go zoom
S tars twinkle out with the moon
T he microphone going boom
A nd generous people smiling without doom
R ocking around, come on, come to the boogie room.

Holly Gibbons (8)
Brampton Junior School

Mepal

M y first impression of Mepal was, *wow!*
E ating my first lunch was tasty
P ractising for our room inspection was funny
A fter our trust trail was archery
L aura was helping us

R aft building was really exciting
E ven we had a race but we lost
S ometimes in the night, Natalie was snoring
I had a great time rock climbing
D oughnuts were really yummy
E ating dinner was good
N ight-time games were really fun
T ime to go to bed
I n the morning it was really cold
A fter snorkelling, time to go home
L ast time on the bus. Time to go home.

Hannah Allan (9)
Brampton Junior School

Mepal

M epal was just as good as I thought
E veryone was having fun and laughing
P addling around in a canoe, having no idea where you are
A rchery was great. I loved the games
L ooking for fish, big and small

R ock climbing, I couldn't get to the top
E ating biscuits and drinking juice halfway through an activity
S ailing I found easy and calm
I also missed my mummy loads
D ucks swimming everywhere
E veryone wet, looking forward to a warm shower
N ext activity, I'm looking forward to it
T owel waiting for me
I want to get home and give my family a hug
A ctivities running around in my brain
L ooking forward to what will happen next.

Jessica Cole (9)
Brampton Junior School

Mepal

M epal was extraordinary
E ating beans on toast was magnificent
P laying on the playscape was exciting
A nd Miss Hughes fell in the lake
L urking round the corner when playing capture the flag was fun

R uari started snoring
E veryone had a wonderful time
S and kept coming in my shoes
I was exhausted on the way back
D angerous or not, a crocodile lives in the lake
E nergy, we needed lots
N ature was a big part
T rust trail was scary
I had a warm shower
A rchery was fun, we played the dating game
L arge trees pass by. I counted 77 football players on the bus - cool!

Cameron Wishart (8)
Brampton Junior School

The Mepal

M y tummy has those butterflies, but I will miss poor Amy
A m eating breakfast, got to be quick
P anicking whether I have my teddy bear
A big, white bus standing in front of me
L ooking at Jessie, we are laughing our heads off

R eally missing my mummy
E nding travelling, get off the bus
S inging lots of merry songs
I think Amy is sad, I felt so sorry for her
D id I really badly want to go?
E at all the food I could, Jessie thought it was revolting!
N ow to see the bedrooms. *Wow!* What a blast!
T owel and wet shoes ready to do snorkelling
I was having so much fun!
A splash of water comes over me
L eaving Mepal can't wait to see my mummy and daddy again!

Jessica Broomfield (9)
Brampton Junior School

Mepal

M epal was fun
E ven though I missed Mum
P leased with my archery
A nd my rock climbing
L oved going to sleep at the end of a long day

R ocking on rocks
E ven when I fell!
S andwiches were yuck!
I n the dorm there was a giant spider
D iving in the lake
E ntering the centre
N atalie was nattering
T om talking
I n his sleep
A nd so did Jimmy
L eaving Mepal in a coach.

Ben Herbert (8)
Brampton Junior School

Mepal

M eeting the instructors and unpacking our bags then
                                exploring everywhere
E ating and drinking, meeting the cook, she was terrifying,
                                but good food
P laying until 9 o'clock, I'm sure we didn't think we would
                                be tired but snoring at 10 o'clock
A ctivities were the best, everyone joining in, people laughing
                                and joking and getting soaked
L ooking grumpy because fun is over, but shattered as ever,
                                but going home to our mums

R eally trying hard at every activity, always trying hard and
                                encouraging people but the main thing was I had fun
E xciting things which happen to me on activities like seeing a pike
S wimming with Miss Hughes on our own, then I swam over
                                to Luke and saw a pike
I n our rooms moving everything around for room inspection
                                so we can get points
D eciding on the food, taking the mick with the cook about beef
E xcited about what the food is, the cook is scary but
                                served lovely food
N ext day, after the first night, it was strange because no school
T he snorkelling glass, you could not breathe out of your nose
                                it was scary at first
I n our rooms people snoring and laughing Miss Hughes
                                saying, 'Sshh!'
A ctivities like our last one was special because it was our last
L eaving was hard, we were depressed and grumpy and tired.

Ryan Son (9)
Brampton Junior School

Grafham Days

A t last we got onto the coach to leave school
B reakfast was delicious
C limbing on the low ropes
D ucking down under nets
E ating an enormous amount of food
F riends in my dormitory Sam, George, David, Jonathan
G eorge was screaming his head off in the night
H aving a lot of fun
I liked orienteering the best
J umping all around
K icking a football all over the field
L unch was very yummy, it sure did fill my tummy
M iss Norman told me about little people indoors
N othing was as exciting as Grafham
O pening lots of dormitories
P aul was wearing very silly trunks
Q uite a lot of people didn't get homesick
R unning with lots of joy
S urfing on the water
T he tuck shop had lots of juicy sweets
U sing an oar to push against the current
V ertically we went up the tower
W alking down walls
X rays I did not need
Y elling when we wanted to come down
Z zzzzzzz I was really tired!

Jack Cooper-Riddiford (7)
Brampton Junior School

Grafham

A ndy was very silly
B iking was fantastic
C anoeing was the best
D ave was a real joker
E venings were the best
F lowing rivers
G rafham rocks
H aving fun is the main part
I enjoyed canoeing the best
J ack was silly
K icking a football was quite good
L ow ropes I enjoyed
M ainly having fun is the best part
N o I did not like windsurfing
O rienteering was with Andy
P aul was very funny
Q uiet, go to sleep exclaimed Miss Norman
R isky bridges in the Grafham challenge
S ailing on the reservoir
T he tuck shop was excellent
U nder the muddy tunnel
V an we went into the mill
W indsurfing was freezing
X rays I did not need
Z zzzzzzzz went to bed.

Samuel Bradshaw-Clifford (8)
Brampton Junior School

The Tulip Fairy

The tulip fairy
Pretty, not scary

Slow and graceful
Sweet and peaceful

The tulip fairy, purple, black and white
As the fairy dances through the starry night

Her dress is made of petals
Now her flower mind begins to settle

As the fairy begins to sleep
The flower kingdom does not make a peep.

Cara Ainsworth (11)
Castle Camps CE Primary School

Roses

Roses are red
None of them are blue.
There are all different kinds
Of roses for you.

Roses have all different colours
They're orange, yellow and white.
They dance about all day
And close up at night.

I like roses, their thorny stem
They have a sweet scent.
They flutter in the wind
And some grow in Kent.

Benjamin Messenger (11)
Castle Camps CE Primary School

The Song Of The Chrysanthemum Fairy

Swaying in the breeze,
Her little bright yellow dress
She sings happy songs.

Her scent is so sweet,
She shares it with everyone,
Just smell her petals.

Her tiny green hat,
Protecting her from the dew,
So silky and smooth.

Smaller than a rose,
But bigger than a daisy,
She sits all alone.

What do they call her?
Chrysanthemum is her name,
Just smell her sweet scent.

Penny Ardley (10)
Castle Camps CE Primary School

Wisteria

My petals are delicate
My flowers are immaculate
Through the evening moon.
The heads are shaded
All silhouetted
In purple, lilac, blue.

I'm a wall-climber
A beauty desire
Flowing over the sky.
My flower's a drooper
The swallow swooper
Is my friend.

Emily Chapman (11)
Castle Camps CE Primary School

Missing You

Even after you've taken one step,
I'll be missing you,
After you've taken five steps,
I'll be missing you,
After you've gone half a mile,
I'll be missing you,
After you're halfway round the world,
I'll still be missing you,
So even when you're standing still,
Or
Walking,
Or
Turning Left,
Or
Right,
I will be missing you!

Jade Bester (11)
Castle Camps CE Primary School

The Song Of The Honeysuckle Fairy

I flitter, I flutter
I fly around all day
I plant my flower, the honeysuckle
But in the evening it's time to play
I play hide-and-seek
With the little honeybees
I try to find a hiding place
So I decide to hide in the trees!
But then I feel a small breeze
I decide it's bedtime for me
I fly home to my little leaf
To become the flower I should be!

Angus Parks (11)
Castle Camps CE Primary School

The Small Begonia Fairy!

I'm the small begonia fairy,
Yes, indeed!
I'm strong, but small
And I grew from a seed!

I'm very shy,
Down near the sea!
30cm is as
Big as I'll be!

My wings are not big,
I can fly also!
I'll stretch and I'll crawl,
Round the garden, I'll go!

Natalie Haylock (10)
Castle Camps CE Primary School

The Horse Chestnut Song

High, high in the sky,
My beautiful flowers lie.
I beside them,
Stroking their stem.
They're white, yellow and pink,
Their petals so pretty they link.
Then baby conkers start to form
And soon the autumn comes, I am forlorn!
My fantastic flowers float away,
Waiting for one day.
After my brother conker has been,
To come back and sit on the tree with me!

Laura Elmer (11)
Castle Camps CE Primary School

The Alpine Fairy's Song

I'm the alpine fairy,
As you can see,
I'm a pretty fairy,
Pretty is me.

I watch all the children,
As they play in the sun.
I wave and I smile
As they have such fun.

I'm the alpine fairy,
As you can see,
I'm a friendly fairy,
Friendly is me.

It's wintertime soon
So I curl up and cry.
Then I lose all my prettiness
And wave life goodbye.

I'm the alpine fairy,
As you can see,
I'm a lovely fairy,
So come, look at me.

Anna Barker (11)
Castle Camps CE Primary School

The English Rose

English rose, dainty and bright,
Upon the world you shine a light,
You cheer up people when they're blue
And cheery people smile at you.

Alas, your thorn brings only tears,
No matter how beautiful you appear,
Oh rose, oh rose, for just one day,
Could you put your thorns away?

Kirsten Goldstone (11)
Castle Camps CE Primary School

The Song Of The Tulip Fairy

I am the tulip fairy,
Colourful and bright,
I come in all different colours,
Red, yellow, purple, pink and white.

I've come all the way from Holland
Just for you
Then you can see my spring colours too.

So however far I've come from
And however far I go
I'm still the little tulip fairy
Everyone knows.

Alice Webb (10)
Castle Camps CE Primary School

What Should I Be?

When I grow up I'm gonna be an astronaut,
No, I don't want to live in space.
When I grow up I'm gonna be a vet,
No, I don't want to work with animals.
When I grow up I'm gonna be a firefighter,
No, red doesn't suit me.
When I grow up I'm gonna be a policewoman,
No, I might injure myself.
When I grow up I'm gonna be a baker,
No, I don't like bread.
When I grow up I'm gonna be a teacher,
No, the kids will drive me crazy.
When I grow up, I know what I'll be . . .
Myself!

Natalie Lemin (11)
Dogsthorpe Junior School

Music Get The Beat

Music get the beat,
Music down your street,
Music in your backyard,
Music isn't hard.
Sing a song,
Sing-a-long,
Music get the beat.
Music in your head,
Music in your bed,
Music in your fingers,
Everywhere it lingers.
Sing a song,
Sing-a-long,
Music get the beat.
Music in the park,
Music after dark,
Music in your cornflakes,
Music as your fishing bait.
Sing a song,
Sing-a-long,
Music get the beat,
Music get the beat,
Yeah!

Fiona Macdonald (10)
Dogsthorpe Junior School

Wings

She had no wings, she could not fly,
In the darkness she would cry.
All day long
And all night through
She cried and cried, she had no clue.

She had no objects, nor anything,
She had no expensive diamond rings,
Because all her life she wanted wings,
She had no time for pretty things.

So one fine day she stood
And came out from under her cloak and hood,
She had a stretch and she spread her wings,
No more did they cling.

Now people stared!
They had no clue,
How happy she was about what she could do!

She is so happy that she can fly
And soar like an eagle way up in the sky,
Her heart is now free and she can now see,
That her wings have set her imagination free.

Charlotte Cooper (11)
Dogsthorpe Junior School

Midnight

The moon's reflection on the sea
Dark and dusty it will be.
No one's out, they're all asleep
Everyone's been counting sheep.
Owls hooting left and right
Come and watch, it's a sight.
Stars are twinkling like a flame
Never put out when it rains.
You can tell when it's midnight.

Melissa Wynne (11)
Dogsthorpe Junior School

Love At First Sight

I love your eyes,
I love your smile,
I cherish your ways,
I adore your style,
But what can I say?
You're one of a kind,
Twenty-four, seven,
You're on my mind.

I know it's hard to see,
I hope you'll agree,
That we're meant to be,
Forever you and me.

Jade Walker (11)
Dogsthorpe Junior School

Girls

Girls are like pearls in your jewellery box
That you treasure forever and a day.
You wrap them in cotton wool to let them know you care
Until you feel the love of a girl
You'll never dare to stray
As her love is like a web
That you'll have to cut free.

Paris Wilson (11)
Dogsthorpe Junior School

Cobra Ways

Slipping, sliding
Through the leaves and trees,
The cobra glides
Through the forest of trees.

Olivier Popple (10)
Dogsthorpe Junior School

The Strange Teacher

The teacher sits on his chair
He gave me a strange little stare.

His round, goofy glasses
Which he looks through as he teaches all the classes.

The children come in
When they hear the school bell ring.

They all start their work
As they saw the teacher lurk.

He started writing names on the board
As they write stories about a lord.

Playtime came
Somebody fell over, they were in pain.

The strange teacher came over
Looking like an ogre!

Sophia Curran (10)
Dogsthorpe Junior School

I've Always Wanted To Go To Space

I've always wanted to go to space
And go and visit the alien race,
I've always wanted to go to the moon,
Sometime around mid-June.
I've always wanted to go to Mars
And go and look at its golden stars,
I've always wanted to see a black hole
And see if it could suck in a spaceship whole!
I've always wanted to go to space
And go and visit the alien race.

Matthew Vernall (10)
Dogsthorpe Junior School

Space

S tars as bright as pearls
P lanets as big as the universe
A liens as scary as your worst nightmare
C omets as big as planets
E erie as the night of a storm.

S tars as white as snow
P lanets red as heat
A liens green and slimy
C omets as big as the Earth
E ars will pop as you get high.

Patrick Newton (10)
Dogsthorpe Junior School

I Wrote Your Name . . .

I wrote your name in the sand,
But the sea washed it away.
I wrote your name in the sky,
But the wind blew it away.
I wrote your name in the snow,
But it got driven away.
I wrote your name in my heart
And forever it will stay.

Jennifer Goodman (10)
Dogsthorpe Junior School

Teachers

Teachers can be cool
Maybe even small
They can have smelly feet
They even overheat
But when it comes to teachers
Telling us the facts
They know when you're putting on an act.

Harriet Musson (11)
Dogsthorpe Junior School

Seaside

I went to the seaside,
I saw a little girl
And in her hair
She had a little curl.

I saw her,
The girl that day,
I called her over
And we went to play.

We went for a swim
At the pool,
She showed me a trick
I thought it was cool.

We went on a donkey,
Across the sand,
She called her mum over,
To hold her hand.

After the donkey ride,
We played with the bucket and spade,
I asked her her name
She said it was Jade.

We went for a picnic,
We ate the food,
Her mum said, 'Time to go in,'
So she got in a mood.

We went to the shops,
To calm herself down,
Then she ran a long way,
All the way back from town.

We went to the fair,
We got some sweets,
We went *wow!*
She got heaps.

Giordan Gregory (10)
Dogsthorpe Junior School

Come Again!

The night is drawn and into dusk.
The wind is blowing loud gusts.
The dark, dark shadows fly past,
Like a cheetah running fast.
The trees are waving.
The houses are gloomy.
Crash! Bang!
What was that?
Crash! Bang!
It's there again.
Oh no, it's starting to rain!
A storm is ahead.
The thunder is banging!
The lightning is crashing!
Wait, it's stopped.
I wonder when it will come again.

Lauren Wood (9)
Dogsthorpe Junior School

The Solar System

Mercury is nearest to the sun,
Venus is still the brightest one,
Earth has lots of blue,
Mars has a reddish hue,
Jupiter is biggest of all,
Gasses swirling in a mighty ball,
Saturn is the father of Jupiter,
Uranus is the father of Saturn,
Neptune is the lord of the sea,
Pluto is the god of the Underworld.

Jannette Taylor (10)
Dogsthorpe Junior School

The Footie World

Football is a great sport,
With the ball, the players and the fouls,
The smelly keeper's towels,
The drink that Beckham drunk,
The kit that really stunk,
The manager's smart suit,
The muddy footie boot,
The keeper blocking the net,
No one has scored yet!

Adam Pettit (9)
Dogsthorpe Junior School

School

Your arms flap,
Some children hop,
Your knees crash,
The chairs drop.

The table tumbles,
Pencil snaps,
The books bounce,
Your arms flap.

Natasha Mohan (10)
Dogsthorpe Junior School

Gorilla

G orillas are fat and hairy
O rang-utans are their near relatives
R ight at rain swinging through the trees
I ce comes and they will hide
L ater on when summer comes they will come out to play
L ight is out and their enemies aren't at bay
A nd now is the time to leave the gorillas in peace.

Patrick Holding (10)
Dogsthorpe Junior School

Football Mad

F ouls are bad
O wn goals are even stupider
O ffside is like a foul but not hurt
T ackle is like stealing the ball away
B all is as round as the moon
A ssistant referee helps the ref when in danger
L inesmen catch people offside
L osers are like a team losing a match

P lay the game of football
L ose the game of football
A ttend the game of football
Y ellow cards
E arn the cup
R ef the game
S uspensions.

Perry Saunders (9)
Dogsthorpe Junior School

The Ocean

The deep, dark, depths,
With old, rotten wrecks.

Then glistening above,
As pure as a dove.

The cool, blue waves
And underground caves.

The reflecting sun shining down on the ocean,
Like a spilt, sparkly potion.

Most of the ocean is blue,
Lots of people like it, do you?

Gabrielle Albert (10)
Dogsthorpe Junior School

Fish

My tank is a coral reef,
Gleaming green, yellow, blue and rainbow,
Every rumble of the ocean is unheard,
Each splash is a hummingbird.

I love to have a share of colour,
Deep as oceans,
Full of motion.

Here are all the colours you could wish,
That's why I'm very fond of fish!

Sarah Chambers (10)
Dogsthorpe Junior School

Giraffe

Giraffe with gentle face
And tall, slender legs,
Like the Eiffel Tower.

Your skin like maps of Africa,
All over your smooth, elegant body.

Your long, towering neck reaches up
For leaves and fruit from the tallest trees.

Your ears are huge,
Like giant leaves sticking out of your face,
Waiting for the slightest sound.

Your eyes peer out,
Like a nosy neighbour.
Your eyelashes pointing out straight,
Like they are gelled.

Your tail looks like a burning, brown torch.
You are *magnificent!*

Robert Wells (11)
Emneth Primary School

The Window

There's a window in a house,
Nothing lives there, except a mouse,
The window has a secret
That no one knows about.

The window has some curtains,
Flowing this way and that,
It is a mess of dirt and cracks
And cobwebs freshly spun.

The window and its secret
Belong in the house,
Do you want to know the secret?
You have to go there to find out.

There's a window in a house,
Nothing lives there, except a mouse,
The window has a secret
That no one knows about.

Emma Barker (11)
Emneth Primary School

Warm Summer Day

Lying still on the grass, napping my eyes,
The breeze blowing through the trees,
Softly rustling as a buzzing bee flies
And soars to do her chores.

A plane in the sky, leaving its trail far behind,
Writing a message all in white
So clear against the celestial blue.

Let me nap and rest in peace,
This tranquil world around me.

William Tysterman (11)
Emneth Primary School

Grey

Dolphins leaping in the air,
Punishing wind blowing across the water with unhappy tears.

Mud, mixing in-between the sand,
Dying and fading, mindful of fires.

People scouring upon the water,
Thinking of what is happening to them.

Saucepans and pots lying in a box,
Crying with oily tears.

Craig Durrant (10)
Emneth Primary School

Butterfly

Butterfly, butterfly, flying high,
Lifting up to touch the blue sky.
Pink, purple, even blue,
These are the beautiful colours of, not me, but you.
Patterns on your coloured wings,
Show us the beauty of what life brings.
Fluttering, fluttering, showing your grace,
Fluttering, fluttering, in your place.

Megan Bywater (11)
Emneth Primary School

The Countryside

The countryside is a deserted town with animals,
It is a blanket that covers millions of acres,
It is a home for millions of new and old tractors,
It is like a supermarket of organic vegetables.

Nathan Ramm (11)
Emneth Primary School

Friends

Friends are very important.

You shouldn't make fun of them,
You shouldn't shout at them,
You shouldn't kick them, punch them
Or hurt them at all,
I did.

You should be kind to them,
You should treat them fairly,
You should give them presents,
Charm bracelets and pots,
I didn't.

Guess what happened?

Genevieve Williams (11)
Emneth Primary School

Love

Love is in the air,
It's trapped inside my heart,
Someone has to free my cares,
Or I'll fall apart.

Love is in the air,
I hope you'll understand,
I love the way you share,
The way you hold my hand.

Love is in the air,
I can feel it up above,
I know I need you there,
So tell me the meaning,
The meaning of love.

Katie Sykes (11)
Emneth Primary School

Falling From Above

Rain is a gentle tap on the window,
Rain is a pounding fist on the roof,
Rain is a gardener watering the flowers,
Rain is a wave surging through cities.

Hail is like golf balls rapping on the roof,
Hail is like cold grey steel whipping your face,
Hail is like a fish trapped in steely nets,
Thrashing about in cold, freezing sweats.

Snow is gentle, twirling in the wind,
Snow is a blanket, white and thick,
Snow floats in flurries, round and round,
Snow piles up around our house.

Rain is a gentle tap on the window,
Rain is a pounding fist on the roof . . .

Luke Goodall (11)
Emneth Primary School

The Wind

The wind goes down.
    Curling, whirling, twisting, whooshing.
        The wind turns round.
            Brushing, crushing, moving, rushing.
                The wind turns up.
                Turning, yearning, churning, learning.
            The wind stops.
        Slowing, showing, people knowing.
    Stopping, stopping, stopping.
As the wind goes down.

Hannah Drewery (11)
Emneth Primary School

Weathers

Snow is gentle, drifting down,
Slowly gathering on the ground.
It falls by day and then by night,
Making a really wonderful sight.

Hail is quickly pelting down,
Howling on our joyful town.
It flies past me and then by you
And it makes a horrid view.

Wind is whistling in the air,
The wind is blowing everywhere.
It blows down river and then down streams,
The wind blows everywhere.

Rain is rippling on the ground
And it makes a funny sound.
In the daytime it is wet,
Until the evening before sunset.

Lee Punter (11)
Emneth Primary School

Subjects

English is OK.
Writing poems is for me,
But stories - not my favourite.
Playing rugby is where I'd rather be.

Maths - now that's the best.
Percentages - I'm a whiz.
But decimals, they turn me off.
I'd rather be doing a quiz.

Science, it's not all that bad.
Circuits, we all enjoy.
But I hate solids, liquids and gases
And so does every girl and boy!

Oliver Porter (10)
Emneth Primary School

Everything To Me!

Sport is everything,
Everything to me.
When I play sports,
I feel so free.

Squash is brilliant,
It's active and cool.
But the bad thing is,
We don't play it at school.

Rugby is the greatest,
The best sport on Earth.
I wish I could have been
There, at the rugby's birth.

Trampolining is wicked,
It's bouncy and high.
If I said I hated it,
I would be telling a lie.

Sport is everything,
Everything to me.
When I play sports,
I feel so free.

Alastair Hardy (11)
Emneth Primary School

Rat

'Rat! Rat! I've just seen a rat!
It's hiding under the kitchen mat!'
'Oh no, what shall we do?
That rat is going to eat you!'
'*Sshh!* Be quiet! It's coming, it's coming . . .
It's coming, to get you!'

'*Squeak! Squeak!*'
'Oh!
It's a *mouse!*'

Monique Harris (11)
Emneth Primary School

The Spider

On a window ledge is where you stay,
Spinning your diamond webs all day.
You stay in gloomy, dark, damp places,
Watching, waiting for familiar faces.

As day disappears, here comes the night,
People start to turn out their light.
No sleep for spider, he's up and away,
You want to know why? You'll find out today.

Morning comes and night-time thins,
This next day will soon begin.
Out comes the primrose sun,
Spider has already had his fun.

As spider reveals his secret ways,
Now you see what he's been doing for days.
You now see his secrets and oh, what a sight!
Another diamond web, laden with lights!

Morgan Ritchie (10)
Emneth Primary School

The Harvest Mouse

It's tiny, its name, Micromys Minutus,
It lives in fields,
It builds . . . fantastic nests . . .
They are the very, very best!
They make them out of grass,
Where the wind blows gently past.
It's shy, it's not very high.

Guess what?
It's a harvest mouse!

Lucy Downham (11)
Emneth Primary School

Stepping Into Mystery

Where will it take me, this long, turning road?
Stepping into somewhere, I do not know.
Can I see the clearing?
Everything is misty -
Fog clinging around the trees -
Hauling and slinging my way.
Leaves damp, branches dangling,
Tangling around me, like a witch's hand.

The trees above turning the world into darkness.
Please let me find my way out -
Trapped in this place of never-ending mystery,
If I call, will anyone hear me?
Oh, road of mystery, lead me safely -
Let me find my way home!

Robert Elcock (11)
Emneth Primary School

Pirates Of The Seven Seas

Yo, ho, ho,
A bottle of rum,
We sail the seven seas.

Yo, ho, ho,
Looking for treasure,
We sail the seven seas.

Yo, ho, ho,
I have only got one leg,
We sail the seven seas.

Yo, ho, ho,
Hang the Devil,
We sail the seven seas.

Jack Edgson (9)
Emneth Primary School

Bugs

B ig
U gly
G ross
S limy

A ggressive
R ubbery
E vil

H orrible
O dd
R idiculous
R evolting
I diotic
D readful!

Abigail Rose (7)
Emneth Primary School

Horses

Horses are the best to ride.
Horses are fast and furry.
Horses are big and miniature.
Horses are noisy and magnificent.
Horses are the best of all!

Rebecca Hanley (9)
Emneth Primary School

Devil Riders

Devil riders are huge,
Devil riders are red,
Devil riders ride devils,
Devil riders are evil,
Devil riders are friends of hobgoblins.

Charlotte Ward (8)
Emneth Primary School

Mr Majeka's Mansion

Mr Majeka's mansion,
Has trapdoors, floors and roof.
Mr Majeka's mansion,
Has many, many toilets.
Mr Majeka's mansion,
Has an ancient Egyptian mummy.
Mr Majeka's mansion,
Has Roman food in the fridge.
Mr Majeka's mansion.

Kieran Jakings (8)
Emneth Primary School

July

In the sun the birds sing
And children play
In the paddling pool in the garden.
What's in the garden?
Flowers;
Tulips, lilies and daisies
And they have petals
And a lovely scent.

Abigail Garrod (8)
Emneth Primary School

Who?

Who is that man I see walking, wandering,
Down by the side of the flowing stream?
Why does he seem not to hear me?
Where does he come from?
What is his name?

Joshua Garrod (11)
Emneth Primary School

The Roman Gets Crushed

Crush, crush, crush,
An elephant on your toes.
Crash, crash, crash,
It will throw you around.
Crush, crush, crush,
Everybody run.
Crash, crash, crash,
Too late.
Crush, crush, crush,
It is raining today.
Crash, crash, crash,
The rain is a pain.
Crush, crush, crush,
You've got to be joking,
I can't live with this!
Send in the god of weather
And ask it gets better!
Crash, crash, crash!
You made it snow,
The elephant is going to die soon.
Crush, crush, crush,
Did you mean die on me? Oh yes,
Crash, crash, crash,
I'll kill you when this elephant gets hold of me.
Crush, crush, crush,
Yeah! The elephant has rotted away.
Crash, crash, crash,
Now, where's that Anglo-Saxon gone?
No more *crash, crush, crash!*

Claire Mead (8)
Emneth Primary School

The Mansion

Down in the deep, dark cell
Is a big ghost
In the shape
Of a bell from Hell . . .

Spooky! Spooky! Spooky!

It is dark
And spiders make webs . . .

Spooky! Spooky! Spooky!

There are the ghosts
Playing on skates . . .

Spooky!

Gemma Cooper (9)
Emneth Primary School

Animals, Animals

Animals, animals in a house,
Who is in there? A little mouse.

Animals, animals in a zoo,
Who is in there? A kangaroo.

Animals, animals in a hole,
Who is in there? A little mole.

Animals, animals with a farmer,
Who is there? A little llama.

Animals, animals everywhere,
Some are quiet and some can scare!

Lisa Williamson (10)
Emneth Primary School

Songbird

Songbird, songbird, you whistle like the wind,
Your feathers are like a rainbow,
Reaching for a note,
You perch outside a house,
Whistling to your heart's content,
Songbird, songbird, you sing with all your heart.

Shanice Moyses (11)
Emneth Primary School

The Spacemen

I have a friend that's a spaceman
He's got a very big tan
He loves it in his space rocket
He says I love it
My arms are still in their socket.

The other spaceman's called Ted
He's got a messed up head
He thinks the TV
Is simply me.

The last one's called Jim
He can't even swim
He gets in the pool
This is cool
But then shouts, 'Get me out!
I want to go to the hall.'

Then me, I'm not a spaceman or silly
I love my dog, Milly
But it's always snoring
He's just boring
I'm learning about space
While I pack my suitcase.

Harry Franklin (8)
Great Abington CP School

The Countryside

The countryside is a place to walk
With silence at my tired feet
As I listen to the birds that tweet
I sit and fall asleep in peace.

I wake up in the mid-day sun
Then put my suncream on
So I don't burn
Still the birds keep on singing.

The day goes on till three
Then I remember about my tea
I run and run as fast as I can
Soon I am home
Just in time for tea
Thinking, *what a wonderful place*
The countryside is!

Karina Brammah (9)
Great Abington CP School

Autumn

Autumn comes and goes,
With a secret, well unknown,
Soft, leafy hails, now unlocked.

Blowing magic breeze,
Summer is consumed and leaves.
Autumn magic comes.

Different colours,
Swirling, whirling, breezes come,
Autumn has to leave.

Winter pushes in,
Frost and snowy gales begin,
Autumn will return.

Evie Haugh (10)
Great Abington CP School

The Night Before Last

The night before last the most magical thing happened . . .
First the sky lit up in an orange blaze
Then shooting stars came down in a golden craze
Next a fire started in the middle of the park
Then, something came out like a bird or a lark
But that was only the beginning . . .

After that, it started to transform into something green and slimy
It looked quite scary even though it was very smiley
It wobbled over and said something strange to me
It was very short and had a big pot-belly
This is when it got a little bit scary . . .

It took my hand and led me into the fire
I thought I was going to be burnt and end up like a sizzly wire
Other aliens just like it, made a circle around me and started to sing
It went something like, tiddle-ong pong ping
This is when it got a bit weird . . .

They each came up to me in turn and bowed their heads
They were green all over but their necks were red
The leader came up holding a watch on a long string
And rocked it gently from side to side
This is when it got a little OTT . . .

My eyes started spinning and I felt dizzy
The world went soaring past and my insides went all fizzy
Before I got carried away
I kicked the leader down to wake another day
This is when they got a bit annoyed . . .
I ran out of the fire
And then they zoomed away
This is when it went quiet.

Antonia Eady (8)
Great Abington CP School

Seaside

Splash! Splash!
Swimming in the sea
I'm playing with my sister
Having a water fight
Let's build a sandcastle
Can I have an ice cream?
Yes.
Lick, lick, lick!

Jordan Raven (9)
Great Abington CP School

The Horse

As the horse stretches her legs
She looks and flings her head
And jumps about and canters.
She's very well behaved
But very fast.
Her ears prick up
And she canters off and away.

Lucy Olivia Edgar (8)
Great Abington CP School

A Sunshine Cinquain

Sunshine,
Warm, warm sunshine,
Golden rays of sunshine,
Warming rays from the boiling sun,
Sunshine.

Penny Malpass (9)
Great Abington CP School

Buying A Pet

Samantha, if you want a cat as a pet,
You shall have to feed it and take it to the vet.

Tom, if you want a dog,
You will have to play with it and throw it a stick or log.

Lilly, if you are really lucky,
I shall go to the pet shop and buy you a puppy.

Jack, if a kitten is your choice,
You will have to not make too much noise.

Polly, if a parrot is what you would like,
Bring it home in a cage on your bike.

Patrick, if a fish is what you want,
Fill its tank from the river front.

'Daisy!' shouted Dad with rage,
'I have told you before, if you want a snake
You should keep it in a cage.'

Billy, now you want a frog,
I am telling you to keep it in a pond near a bog.

Josie, if you *really* want a rabbit,
At breakfast, lunch and supper, give it a carrot.

Dave? Getting a crocodile?
Yes, he said he'd keep it in a cage,
Over a stream with pictures of the River Nile.

Isabella, a mouse? No I said a hamster would be great!

Pleeeease get one for me when I am eight!

Christopher Nightingale (8)
Great Abington CP School

Favourite Things

Amy's favourite thing is a bee.
Mine is simply, simply me.
Charlie's favourite thing is air.
Robin and Lucy's are their teddy bears.
Favourite things are everywhere.
Everywhere, everywhere.

Anna's favourite thing's her pet.
James belongs to the vet.
Sian's favourite thing's a song.
Sam's is to stay in bed long.
Favourite things are everywhere.
Everywhere, everywhere.

Emily's favourite thing's a horse.
The shining hair bobble belongs to Dorse.
Paul's favourite thing's his knife.
Polly's is her long, long life.
Favourite things are everywhere.
Everywhere, everywhere.

Alice Merryweather (8)
Great Abington CP School

Come!

Come on,
Let's go see,
The birds sing,
In the polluted tree.
So come on,
Let's go help.

Hannah Malpass (9)
Great Abington CP School

Football

I love football
I've liked it since
I was a second old.
I started with a small ball
To score a goal.

My friends were mad on football too.
Mick kicked
Dave saved.
Every day we would
Go out and play.

For my fifth birthday
I called for a big ball.
Twenty years later
I'm at Wembley
Scoring a hat-trick
Because my name's Patrick.

Fifty years later
My grandsons lay
So I'll teach them how to play.

Charlie Froment (8)
Great Abington CP School

Sweets

Toffee, caramel and chocolate treats
And things you would really like to eat.
I love sweets, a creamy egg, a toffee bar
I love cakes, a cake in the shape of a car.
I like sweets!

Jessica Howe (8)
Great Abington CP School

Writing A Poem

Writing a poem is ever so hard,
I don't know what sort to do.
I can only think of a shape poem,
Or maybe a tanka or haiku.

But the thing I mostly get stuck on,
Is what to write a poem about.
School, space, families, feelings,
Or maybe just a pig's snout.

There are so many different types of poems,
I don't know what to do.
So I thought and thought
And came up with this one for you.

Alex Taylor (9)
Great Abington CP School

My Cousin's Little Dog

My cousin's got a little dog
And she always throws it a stick or log
My cousin's got a little dog
She takes it in the sun
And all day long they have fun.

My cousin's got a little dog
It cries and weeps
And never sleeps
My cousin's got a little dog
When he's in his bed
He always plays with a spider's web.

Robyn Hammond (8)
Great Abington CP School

Echoes

Once I saw the north wind
In a room swirling round a tree,
I shouted out a funny name
It shouted back to me.

I got scared and walked off
My footsteps trailed behind,
But then a scary thought
Made its way into my mind.

I stopped and looked back
But there was nothing there,
It must have been some echoes
Wandering through the air.

Stacy Drieu (9)
Great Abington CP School

Dreams

Dreams are the heart of us
Dreams are us
Dreams we like
Dreams we don't forget
Dreams can be anything

Life means nothing without dreams
Our soul is our dreams

Dreams, dreams, dreams, dreams, dreams
Are our soul.

James Harrison (9)
Great Abington CP School

Bumblebee

Bumblebee, bumblebee
Don't be afraid
Bumblebee, bumblebee
Go in the shade.

Bumblebee, bumblebee
Please go away
Bumblebee, bumblebee
Please do it . . .
Today!

Anna Krylander (9)
Great Abington CP School

A Feather

Floating down without a sound
Swiftly swirling to the ground
Letting everyone see
How beautiful a feather can be
So if you ever see a feather
Just watch it float towards you and realise
How beautiful they can really be.

Rachael Cornwell (9)
Great Abington CP School

Teachers

Teachers, teachers do maths with you
Teachers, teachers they always say, 'Boo!'
Teachers, teachers they're all fun
Teachers, teachers let you play in the sun
Teachers, teachers when it's dark
Teachers, teachers let you go to the park.

Evie Roddom (7)
Great Abington CP School

The Wicked Witch!

Her nose as crooked as a twisted twig,
Her hair as knotted as seaweed,
Her teeth as black as night,
Her ugly hands as stiff as a table.

Her back as bony as a skeleton,
Mixing a random potion,
Laughing an evil laugh,
Chin as pointed as a sharp pencil.

Her clothes as small as a goldfish,
Her nose sniffing all the smells in the world,
Her tongue as ugly as a frog,
Her eyes as green as grass.

Emily Bugg (9)
Holme CE Primary School

The Golden Streak

Gliding over the cliff
He spots his prey.

He shoots down like a golden streak
Silhouetted against the sky.

Feathers flapping in the breeze
He pulls up just before he hits the ground
He clamps a mouse in his beak
Then back to the nest he goes.

While he's flying, five other birds join him
All zooming, feathers fluttering in the wind
Go the golden eagles.

Alexander Collins (9)
Holme CE Primary School

The Forest

A misty, gloomy forest,
Has a never-ending view,
With white and grey,
Foggy streams,
With the trees that sway
In the breeze.

Cold and gloomy forest,
Has a spark of lightning,
As the rustling leaves
Crunch as footsteps walk
Along in the foggy mist,
To the howling sound of wind
And rain trickling down.

Molly Edwards (10)
Holme CE Primary School

Winter Wonderland

I am a tree, I whistle and glisten,
My bushes blow and glow.
When it is time, my leaves fall,
The bears scratch their fur.
When it is windy, I wobble,
My branches straight as soldiers.
The trees tower together.
My view is beautiful.
Friendless blue sky,
The clouds are clear and creamy white.
The owls hoot.

Abigail Tandy (10)
Holme CE Primary School

The Winter Forest

As the night rolls in,
The moon will glow.
When the owls fly,
The wind will blow.

Twisting fingers viciously grabbing,
The tall, spidering figures of the night,
Whispering secrets in the wind,
Then the darkness turns into twilight.

Laura Davies (11)
Holme CE Primary School

The Hope Of War

Grief-laden
A palace of despair
Hallways of stone and sadness
Then a window filled with hope
Spreading and growing
The white light of horse and rider
Shining with the hope of dawn
Just enough to ride out and face the servants of evil.

Adam Spratley (11)
Holme CE Primary School

The Wicked Witch

The witch flew through the air like an aeroplane at top speed.
Her cloak trailed behind her like a wedding dress.
Her nose was as sharp as a knife.
She was as thin as a twig.
Her top and skirt were as silver as the stars.

Gemma Custance (9)
Holme CE Primary School

The Winter Wood

The shattered oak
Enclosed in the lair of the winter wood
The gnarled branches
Reaching out with their twisted fingers
Viciously hurling towards me
Haunted, bewildered
Mysteriously blowing back and forth
Slender twigs, hidden under the limp, crisp leaves
Eyeing me carefully with their menacing knots
Are the towering trees of the winter wood
The querulous wind threads through the branches
Perilous trees stand grandiose as soldiers
Rotting bark opening and closing like a dilapidated door
Silence . . .
The desolation spreads through the entire wood
Nevertheless
The whisper of the breeze continues
How still, how calm
And life goes on in the winter wood.

Leilani Barratt (9)
Holme CE Primary School

Trees Of The Midnight World

Damp, depressing sights
From the skeletons of trees
In the midnight frost.

In the winter breeze
The trees sway
Grey leaves falling on the floor.

Rustling noises all around
Shadows made by the midnight moon
There they are, the trees of the midnight world.

Bethany Wilkins (11)
Holme CE Primary School

The Drum

Can you hear the drum playing?
The beats are words but what is it saying?
Booming notes are loud and clear,
Through its skin and in my ear.

People will be dancing,
Jumping and prancing,
Rhythmic notes, short and long,
Boom bada, boom bada, bada bong.

Animals swaying in a hypnotic trance,
Lions and cheetahs start to advance,
All of them roaming free,
Hearts content as they can be.

It speaks to me,
Setting souls free,
Fears are shifted,
People's hearts are lifted.

Lucy Walters (11)
Holme CE Primary School

Terrifying Trees

Thin, bare trees stand alone in the misty winter forest.
Leaves slowly drift towards the earth.
Rotten logs lie cold on the ground.
Trees quiver in fear of the frost to come.
Towering trees, gnarled and ragged, viciously grabbing.
Gloomy skies circling above.
Trees spiraling towards the sky, trying to breathe.

Amelia Tillson-Smith (11)
Holme CE Primary School

The War Of Hope

Desperate men hack at relentless Uruk-hai,
Lifeless corpses litter the ground,
Heroic men give up all hope of life.

The young men shaking,
Out of fear and death,
As rain dampens their spirits.

Grief-laden women praying,
As constant thuds of feet
And blood-curdling screams,
Rip the silence of the caves.

Dawn creeps near,
Bringing more hope to men and elves
And death for all Uruk-hai.

Martha Cattell (11)
Holme CE Primary School

The Warriors' Hope

When war is upon you
And you go to fight
Your hours are being counted down
But don't give up
Or lose all hope
For life will conquer death
For good will conquer evil
However deadly or warmongering
Your enemy might be
Or however many there are
For light, like hope, never dies
But only moves away
And so after the darkest hour
Hope will come again.

Stuart Rennie (10)
Holme CE Primary School

A Terrible Fate

The horns that blew
Are no more
All hope was destroyed

The world is black with hate
Courage is fading
The race of men is falling

The wall has been breeched
The fort is destroyed
All hope has gone
For the king.

Philip Spriggs (10)
Holme CE Primary School

Athena

A thena
T he master of all questions
H era and Zeus' daughter
E verlasting wisdom and strength
N ever afraid or shy
A lways meant to fight and hate

I ntelligent
S lain many things

W ith many weapons
I t would be a terrible thing to meet her
S he will hack at anything moving
D eath is her entertainment
O ther things are boring
M any people fear her.

Sam Dane (10)
Longthorpe Primary School

Zeus, King Of The Gods

Z eus
E ver powerful
U nderneath his veins give him power
S o mighty

K ing of everything
I n his kingdom he is very powerful
N ow he is remembered by the Greeks
G od of all gods

O ver the clouds controlling Heaven
F amous everywhere

A ll praise Him
L iving on Mount Olympus
L uxurious Greece

G reece, a very big country
O lympus, Zeus' home
D eadly thunderbolts
S torms are what Zeus controls.

Leon Hamid Ouardighi (10)
Longthorpe Primary School

Zeus

Z eus is the king of gods and goddesses
E ven he is so strong
U nder the ground he has a brother called Hades
S upreme ruler of the Olympian dynasty was Zeus.

Trevena Bisla (9)
Longthorpe Primary School

Zeus

Z eus
E ver powerful
U nderneath he is peaceful
S o mighty

K ing of the gods
I ndestructable
N ever will he die
G uarding Mount Olympus

O ver Mount Olympus he reigns king
F or all the Greek people

G reece bows down to him
O ver the clouds is what he controls
D eadly thunderbolts he throws
S torms are what he rules.

Ross Symns (10)
Longthorpe Primary School

Zeus

K ing of gods,
I n the sky,
N obody disobeys him,
G od who throws lightning bolts.

O n Mount Olympus,
F or that's where he lives.

G od of sky, storms, lightning and thunder,
O ver the weather he rules,
D ad to Hercules,
S on of Cronus.

Abby Calderbank (10)
Longthorpe Primary School

Zeus

Z eus, king of the gods and goddesses,
E very day he fights,
U sually he fights really difficult people,
S ometimes he is in big danger.

A t night he would still travel,
N ever stopping,
D ay after day as well.

H urting at every step,
I t was hard running and walking,
S topping to take a breath.

F eeling awful for what he did,
A lways feeling sorry,
M emories for what he did,
I t was hard to talk,
L imping everywhere
Y elling for help.

Monique Williams (9)
Longthorpe Primary School

Goddess Hera

Goddess Hera up above,
Sparkling dresses with a dove.
Zeus's wife, queen of Heaven,
Hera's favourite, number seven.
Hera's voice, hear her sound,
In Heaven she'll always be found.
Sitting on clouds,
Singing out loud,
Celebrating and enjoyable,
People know she's reliable.

Rebecca Jones (10)
Longthorpe Primary School

Zeus

Zeus, ruler of all Heaven,
Supreme king of all the world,
Worshipped by mortals,
An unstoppable force.

Zeus,
Brother to the most powerful gods,
Married to Hera,
Son of the almighty Cronus.

Zeus,
Destroyer of the Titans,
He banished them,
Crushed them,
Amazing he is.

Reza Petersen (10)
Longthorpe Primary School

Oh, Zeus

Zeus is king of the gods
Ruler of Heaven and clouds
Controller of sky and universe
Protector of family and friends.

Zeus, father of Hercules
Husband of Hera
Brother of Poseidon
Rhea's eldest son.

Zeus, killer of Crosnos
Protecting Mount Olympus
Watching the Olympics
Oh, Zeus.

James Lovell (9)
Longthorpe Primary School

Zeus

Zeus, the king of gods,
Ruler of kings,
Controller of weather,
Protector of people,
Supreme he was!

Zeus, son of Cronus,
Brother of Poseidon and Hades,
Father of Hercules,
Husband of Hera,
A mighty family he had!

Zeus fought many battles,
He fought Titans,
Destroyed them,
Banished them,
To the Tartarus,
Mighty he was!

Famous all over Greece,
Awarded with festivals,
Temples built to him,
Worshipped all around,
Heroic he was!

Michael Russell (10)
Longthorpe Primary School

Athena

Athena, goddess of wisdom
Athena, daughter of Zeus
Athena, the motherless girl

Athena, the problem solver
Athena, Athens creator
Athena, a young woman.

Hannah Sharman (10)
Longthorpe Primary School

A Poem About Zeus

Zeus is the ruler of them all
He is strong, wise and ruler of the heavens
Zeus is unafraid and powerful
Zeus's wife is Hera
She is the goddess of wisdom
All the gods live on Mount Olympus
But Zeus is the strongest of them all.

Zeus is the god of Heaven
He could tell what people were thinking before they could
Zeus, Zeus, powerful, strong and wise
Zeus is the ruler of them all
Zeus, Zeus, Zeus, the most powerful
Zeus is strong
Zeus is wise
Zeus, Zeus, Zeus, Zeus, Zeus.

Charlie Ding (9)
Longthorpe Primary School

Hephaestus

H ephaestus is the god of fire
E veryone picked on him
P eople beat him up as well
H e got thrown in the sea
A nd got saved by the nymphs
E very day he wanted revenge
S uddenly Hephaestus got stronger and stronger
T he next day Hephaestus was going to attack
U sing a great big axe
S o he attacked and got his revenge.

Ashley Watson (10)
Longthorpe Primary School

Athena

G oddess of wisdom,
O wl - her symbol of wisdom,
D ressed with a shield and helmet,
D evoted her love to Mymex,
E ventually turned her into an ant,
S word she is holding,
S he was born in an unusual way.

A thena coming out of Zeus' head,
T ries not to fall in loves with males,
H era's daughter,
E verlasting wisdom,
N ever underestimating people,
A thena, a beautiful woman.

Iram Hussain (10)
Longthorpe Primary School

Athena

G oddess of wisdom and marriage,
O wl is her symbol,
D oesn't fall in love,
D aughter of Zeus,
E verlasting power,
S he wears a helmet,
S he holds a shield.

A thena is a young woman,
T urned Myrmex into an ant,
H ead birth,
E verlasting of wisdom,
N ever had children,
A thena's mum is Hera.

Christina Mudge (10)
Longthorpe Primary School

Hades Poem

Hades, king of the underworld,
Master of the dead,
Stealer of Persephone,
Maker of the unhappiness of Demeter.

Brother of Zeus and Poseidon,
Married to Persephone,
Rider of a black chariot,
Owner of a three-headed dog.

Known as the god of wealth,
Pluto is named after him,
Fierce and inexorable god,
Son of Olympus.

Lizzie Mallett (10)
Longthorpe Primary School

Athena Is Zeus' Favourite Daughter

Athena is the daughter of Zeus,
She is the god of wisdom,
She came out of her father's head
Singing a song,
She was Zeus' favourite daughter.

Athens is named after Athena,
She invented useful things like the trumpet,
She played a big role in some Greek lives,
She was Zeus' favourite daughter.

Jennifer Chaney (10)
Longthorpe Primary School

Athena

Athena, the most important god,
Helping so many Greeks,
Wearing armour as she goes,
Skilled in many things,
Born out of her father's head.

Athena, daughter of Zeus,
She never married or had a love,
Goddess of wisdom and craft,
Zeus' favourite daughter,
She invented many useful things,
Like the flute and the trumpet.

Athena, the most important of all goddesses!

Becky Stevenson (10)
Longthorpe Primary School

Zeus

Zeus, one of the seven wonders of the world,
The most supreme god of Olympus,
Married to Athena the goddess of wisdom,
Lived on Mount Olympus,
The most magnificent powers.
Son of Cronus and Rhea,
The father of Hercules,
Husband of Hera,
Killed his own father.
Knew what people were thinking before they did,
The leader of all gods,
The greatest Greek god.

Ahkeel Mahmood (10)
Longthorpe Primary School

England Rugby Ballad

Once in early October,
England won as I do well remember,
Twelve trys were scored,
In the month of September,
In the month of September.

We travelled forth towards the cup,
Speeding all the way,
One try was scored,
Wilko is the best they say,
Wilko is the best they say.

A little man is Robinson,
He got an MBE,
He scored a try,
Then was never seen,
Then was never seen.

Wilko kicked a drop goal,
And was playing in fly-half,
He took seventeen conversions
And charged at them like a calf,
And charged at them like a calf.

Martin is a big man,
Two hundred centimeters tall,
He charges like a rhino
And takes every single ball,
And takes every single ball.

Will is very fast
And has scored thirty trys,
He normally plays in centre
And gives out a lot of cries,
And gives out a lot of cries.

So with our team going ahead,
It is the beginning of a campaign,
We won 20-17,
Then opened a bottle of champagne,
Then opened a bottle of champagne.

Joshua Fenttiman (10)
Perse Preparatory School

Ballad Of Yuri Gagarin

A thing was done in 61
That changed mankind forever
Yuri Gagarin, in a tube of tin
Felt as light as a feather
Felt as light as a feather

In *Vostok 1* he went towards the sun
He went up to orbit Earth
As Russia's ace, in the great space race
He brought a new age to birth
He brought a new age to birth

The Earth he found, when off the ground
Was gigantic, round and blue
In orbit one, around he spun
And watched the amazing view
And watched the amazing view

He wasn't late in 108
Minutes of his flight
All the way, around the day
And right the way round the night
And right the way round the night

He landed again, on the Russian plain
With a great big thud, not a splash
As a hero overnight, because of his flight
But died in a terrible crash
But died in a terrible crash.

Thomas Myers (10)
Perse Preparatory School

The Ballad Of The Marathon

The Persians were on the rampage,
Conquering all the land that they could,
They were building up their empire,
And the warriors thought themselves good,
And the warriors thought themselves good.

Their next target was Athens,
But they hadn't got to it yet,
They had only got to Marathon,
But what a surprise they were going to get,
But what a surprise they were going to get!

For the Athenians knew they were coming,
And sent me, Phidippedes, for aid,
I had to ask the Spartans to join us,
Otherwise all our men would be slayed,
Otherwise all our men would be slayed.

It was to be a 140-mile run,
To get help was the only cause,
But they said they wouldn't help us till the next full moon,
Due to religious laws,
Due to religious laws.

Then I had to run all the way back,
All the way back to Athens,
I told them that the Spartans had refused,
Because of lunar patterns,
Because of lunar patterns.

So the Athenians and I set off for Marathon,
All on our own,
To try and ambush the Persians,
We were all scared to the bone,
We were all scared to the bone!

Some thought it was suicide,
But all the warriors were brave,
And didn't care if the Persians killed them,
Sending them to an early grave,
Sending them to an early grave.

We had now reached Marathon,
And the Persians were in sight,
Everyone raised their swords and spears,
They were all preparing for a fight,
They were all preparing for a fight.

The battle was big and bloody,
The Athenians were outnumbered four to one,
But somehow the Persians were defeated,
Finally the battle was done,
Finally the battle was done.

Some surviving Persians fled to sea,
And headed south towards my hometown,
I knew that I had to run all the 26 miles back,
But when it comes to running I'm the man in the crown,
But when it comes to running I'm the man in the crown.

I got back to Athens and told them the news,
Of the Persians coming to conquer,
I also told them about the victory,
Then I felt my head go bonk-a,
Then I felt my head go bonk-a.

I don't know what happened,
I think I had just fallen down and died,
Probably from exhaustion,
On the way up to Heaven I cried,
On the way up to Heaven I cried.

Now I am up above,
Looking down on Earth,
Seeing people running 26-mile marathons,
Of which I was the birth,
Of which I was the birth.

David Meredith (10)
Perse Preparatory School

The Ballad Of England Winning The World Cup 1966

Some years back in sixty-six
As my folks do well remember
It was some day the 30th of July
Some day to remember
Some day to remember

We went through some tough days
Under the hot sun
It took some energy
To beat the Hun
To beat the Hun

Geoff Hurst the hero
Under that sun
Scored that goal
That put out the Hun
That put out the Hun

They beat the Portugesa
In the semi-final
On a memorable day
The fans at home listened on wireless
The fans at home listened on wireless

Bobby Moore was captain in that fairy tale
The golden trophy theirs at last
All Germans' faces turned pale
Great memories of that time now all in the past
Great memories of that time now all in the past.

Jonathan Butler (10)
Perse Preparatory School

The Ballad Of Stamford Bridge

In the year of 1066,
A fleet of 300 ships-a,
Sailed down-a our River Humber,
And marched on towards the great Stamford Bridge-a,
And marched on towards the great Stamford Bridge-a.

Across the bridge they strode,
12 brave English men,
As hostages they came across without a falter, as they were
Fearing a slaughter,
To save many a man,
To save many a man.

Surprised good King Harold rushed
And marched to York in just five days,
The English crossed, the hostages remained in a dither,
The Norwegians all fell that day,
The Norwegians all fell that day.

King Harold advanced forward,
Into Orri's storm,
Beating the Vikings slowly,
Into a battered form,
Into a battered form.

The Vikings twice were offered surrender,
Twice it was refused,
24 of the 300 returned to the startled hundreds,
The Vikings returned confused,
The Vikings returned confused.

Our good King Harold,
Defended Hastings,
And fell there too,
He fell to William's sting,
He fell to William's sting.

Edward Noble (10)
Perse Preparatory School

A Ballad Of Jack The Ripper

Some years of late in eighty-eight,
It was a shining moon,
It was, some say, the start of May
And ended on a June,
And ended on a June.

Jack the Ripper
The uncaught killer,
Who struck terror in London's East End,
Seven were killed and quickly unfilled,
Seven were killed and quickly unfilled.

The seven women
And the last victim,
Were throat-slashed with a sharp knife,
Some said a scalpel and a sharp scythe,
Some said a scalpel and a sharp scythe.

Investigations by Scotland yard,
London's Metropolitan police,
Were finally brought to one of the ends,
That they thought would never cease,
That they thought would never cease.

Jack the Ripper
An uncaught killer,
Was hanged and buried a-dead,
Then he took one last look before he was never again fed,
Then he took one last look before he was never again fed.

Ryan Anand (9)
Perse Preparatory School

The Ballad Of The Gunpowder Plot

A long while ago in 1603,
Queen Elizabeth died,
It was, some say, the 2nd of May,
But most do not remember,
But most do not remember.

James the 1st became the king,
But many people hated him,
The Catholics were angry
And wanted to be rid of him,
And wanted to be rid of him.

Robert Catsby rallied a band,
To kill their evil king,
There was a young man called Guy Fawkes,
Listen as I sing,
Listen as I sing.

Robert rented a cellar,
Under the House of Lords,
He used two tons of gunpowder
And fused it using cords,
And fused it using cords.

In their band there was a coward,
Whose friend would be there on that night,
He wanted to warn him,
He didn't want to kill him,
He didn't want to kill him.

So in the end their plan was foiled,
And Parliament didn't blow,
Catsby was shot
And Guy was hung, drawn and quartered
And Guy was hung, drawn and quartered.

James Hopkin (10)
Perse Preparatory School

Orford Castle 'The Ballad'

A few years back in 1176,
The defences grand, all attackers ooer,
The castle took three year to build,
King Henry II did build her,
King Henry II did build her.

With all the royal visits, she was very grand,
Orford Castle, aye is nowhere near Dover,
Under Henry's command we attack,
We bowl all barons over,
We bowl all barons over.

Orford had all the requirements,
Water and the servants' quarter,
Bakery 'n' all,
A very good quality dining quarter,
A very good quality dining quarter.

Built with bricks, stone an' wood,
Three a privy she did have-a,
Built on sandy earth,
Home-made bread taste nice-a,
Home-made bread taste nice-a.

Lunch in the Great Hall, King and all,
Storytellers the criminals heard,
High ceilings everywhere, no spies we ever saw,
Prison cells up high, how absurd,
Prison cells up high, how absurd.

Nicholas Lander (10)
Perse Preparatory School

The Ballad Of The Great Wall Of China

Some years of late, in sixty-eight,
Some monks decided fairly,
It was exactly as I thought,
The start of January,
The start of January.

The Chinese men built their Great Wall,
Around their country, China,
They said it was invincible,
And also said it was fine-a,
And also said it was fine-a.

It was the longest structure built,
About 4,000 miles long,
And was entirely made by hand,
And it is said to be quite strong,
And it is said to be quite strong.

The one Great Wall was sometimes called,
It was also known as 'The Long Graveyard',
For many people died whilst building this,
For it was extremely hard,
For it was extremely hard.

The Wall of China was actually built,
For the purpose of defence,
But now it lies in ruins,
And is just like a fence,
And is just like a fence.

Nicholas Li (9)
Perse Preparatory School

A Ballad Of The Abominable Snowman

A young man of 22, didn't know what to do,
He decided to go to Asia,
He didn't know the date, and he left late,
Into the Himalaya,
Into the Himalaya.

He went into a mountain, and he found a fountain,
He then spotted birds, a flock,
The birds looked at he, as he could see,
And then, he moved a rock,
And then, he moved a rock.

The rock he took, and out came a rook,
Which pecked him on the head,
A shape came out, and the rook flew about,
He thought, 'Soon I'll be dead,'
He thought, 'Soon I'll be dead.'

The enormous shape, looked like an ape,
It was tall as a big bike,
It turned to leave, and ripped his sleeve,
The beast looked hairy man-like,
The beast looked hairy man-like.

When it had gone, the sunlight shone,
He shouted, 'Yahoo man,'
His name was Rory, he told his story,
'I've seen the abominable snowman,
I've seen the abominable snowman.'

Robert Lowther   (10)
Perse Preparatory School

The Ballad Of The Dinosaurs Getting Wiped Out

A herd of diplodocus steadily graze
The allossaurus' heads slowly raise
They are hunting their prey
They have been behind them all day
They have been behind them all day

The pack split the grazers and youngster was caught
The diplodocus fell and the herd was fraught
The sky explodes and crackles with light
Even though it is as dark as midnight
Even though it is as dark as midnight

A massive wind came before the storm
The meteors rained down and all was torn
Then the huge rock smashed into the Earth
And all was blotted out as it shattered its girth
And all was blotted out as it shattered its girth.

The dinosaurs died in the dust cloud that blew
And a tidal wave hit and all live died too
The dinosaur bones are all lying at rest
Is there a dinosaur left in Loch Ness?
Is there a dinosaur left in Loch Ness?

William Harris (10)
Perse Preparatory School

What Do You Suppose?

What do you suppose?
A bee sat on my nose!
Then what do you think?
He gave me a wink!
He said, 'I beg your pardon,
I thought you were the garden!'

Howard Danner (8)
Perse Preparatory School

A Ballad Of The Iraq War

In March of two thousand and three,
The war in Iraq started.
Americans and British went,
To Iraq they departed,
To Iraq they departed.

George Bush wanted to catch Saddam,
Americans were behind him,
And Tony Blair was with him too,
Though the UN thought it was dim,
Though the UN thought it was dim.

In the desert soldiers stood,
Some in Iraq some out of it,
Some of them didn't seem to care,
As all they would do was sit,
As all they would do was sit.

The BBC would get the news,
Far braver than the soldiers,
That's what the reporters were,
Them and the camera holders,
Them and the camera holders.

Saddam was still at large,
George Bush he saw no point,
And neither did Tony Blair,
So their two forces joint,
So their two forces joint.

They attacked many places,
Baghdad, Basra, Tikrit,
If they found a thing that just might help,
Then with them they would take it,
Then with them they would take it.

Some Iraqis turned against Saddam,
And statues would have fallen,
And anything else to praise Saddam,
The Iraqis would destroy 'em,
The Iraqis would destroy 'em.

Near Tikrit they found Saddam,
Far, far from the town's soul,
He wasn't trying to destroy us,
But hiding in a hole,
But hiding in a hole.

Saddam was finally taken in,
And many tests were taken,
The news was heard across the world,
And his supporters shaken,
And his supporters shaken.

Christopher Littlefair (10)
Perse Preparatory School

The Wind

Feel the wind up in the trees,
Come along and follow me.
Feel its song, its melody,
It makes you feel that you are free.
From the mountains,
To the valleys,
From sea to shining sea,
Hear the song,
Its melody,
And now,
Come,
With,
Me.

Tom Norris (11)
Perse Preparatory School

The Ballad Of The Mary Rose

She was born in 1509,
And died 34 years later,
She lived a long and bloody life,
She lived a long and bloody life.

As she sailed the sea so far,
She defended the sailors right down to their toes-a,
How she did it, nobody knows-a,
How she did it, nobody knows-a.

In this ballad I have written,
That she was the defence of our land Britain,
She served us well and did us good,
For should we be grateful? Yes we should,
For should we be grateful? Yes we should.

As the Scots and French came near,
Their guns were too loud for us to hear,
The Rose was in trouble, so were we,
The rose was in trouble, so were we.

But yes, the Rose just had to come down-a,
And no more was there a sound-a,
But we remember the lives she saved,
But we remember the lives she saved.

Eddie Addo (10)
Perse Preparatory School

Dunkirk

Some years declined in '39,
As I do well remember,
Some say it was 12th of May,
And some say, in September,
And some say, in September.

Adolf Hitler ordered an invasion to France,
With allies of 1,400,
Supported by Belgian and British,
In total of 1,250 divisions and 3,000 tanks,
In total of 1,250 divisions and 3,000 tanks.

By air French dominated, but on land Germany lost,
What a bloody war-a,
144,000 left in the French army,
The rest had died-a,
The rest had died-a.

Now England stood alone,
And were outnumbered-a,
With groups of two hundred dotted everywhere,
And we retreated,
And we retreated.

Alex Pak (10)
Perse Preparatory School

Ready

Wash your face,
Brush your hair,
Clean your teeth,
Get dressed,
But don't forget your thermal vest.
We're going to be late,
We're going to be late,
So be quick and clear your plate.
What are we going to do?
What *are* we going to do?
Help, quickly, I need the loo.
Okay, here we go,
Is everyone ready?
Oh sorry, I forgot my teddy.
Don't you feel that every day,
When you and your brother visit Aunty May,
Getting ready is such a bore
And that every time,
There is more and more?

Thomas Reynolds (8)
Perse Preparatory School

Vultures

The vulture is a bulky bird,
When it hops it looks quite absurd.
With huge wings and massive eyes,
It hunts animals that have already died.
It twists and turns in the thermals.
When it sees its prey, it slowly circles down,
Then it goes *munch, crunch, crunch.*

Andrew Green (7)
Perse Preparatory School

The Ballad Of Flying The Flyer

In days of old so I am told
There were two brothers Wright.
They had a vision, a premonition
To be the first in flight
To be the first in flight.

They tested gliders and tested kites
They worked and worked through many a night.
They did their sums, they planned their flight
But were their calculations right?
But were their calculations right?

At last in December 1903
There occurred a wondrous sight.
In North Carolina they came to see
At Kitty Hawk the world's first flight
At Kitty Hawk the world's first flight.

120 feet they flew
The amazement grew and grew.
Orville and Wilbur Wright
Accomplished the first ever flight
Accomplished the first ever flight.

On Kill Devil Hill
They knew not how soon
From this beginning
Man would fly to the moon!
Man would fly to the moon!

Angus Osborn (10)
Perse Preparatory School

The Ballad Of Dunkirk

In late May and early June in 1942
Events took place
Which changed the face
Of all of World War II
Of all of World War II

So the men they marched
From Northern France
And hollered as loud as they could
Away, away back to the beaches
Away, away back to the beaches

So Hitler he asked for surrender
And decided to pause the agenda
The fool he thought it was over
But Britain had a plan
But Britain had a plan

So in they sent the cavalry
To rescue them from purgatory
Men in dinghies, yachts and sloops
Gave help with Britain's naval troops
To rescue back the boys
To rescue back the boys

So when you hear of Dunkirk spirit
Don't you forget this little lyric
Britain had its finest hour
A national pride new to flower
A national pride new to flower.

Max Palmer-Geaves (10)
Perse Preparatory School

The Ballad Of The French Revolution

Some say the French are merciful
Some say the French are bad
But those who said the first option
Will wish they never had
Will wish they never had

The cruel king called Louis
Raised the tax of bread
While the people in the fields
Had a price upon his head
Had a price upon his head

A man called Jean-Paul
Rose up above the rest
He never rested till t'was done
And Louis was in a chest
And Louis was in a chest

The Austrians came and saw
The French were in a panic
They came down prepared for war
And the French were so frantic
And the French were so frantic

Napoleon stepped he up
And they went into battle
The French needed soldiers more
All as hard as cattle
All as hard as cattle

Into the bloodbath they all went
And fought with tooth and claw
While Jean-Paul got the chop
And he rebelled no more
And he rebelled no more.

Jamie Seaward (10)
Perse Preparatory School

The Ballad Of The Battle Of Hastings

In the latter months of sixty-six,
October or September,
So long ago, one thousand years!
That no one can remember,
That no one can remember.

Harold the king had war with the duke,
William of Normandy,
The war took place, north of Hastings,
In the bay of Pevensey,
In the bay of Pevensey.

William wanted to conquer,
England so that he
Could become king of England and
Not just Duke of Normandy,
Not just Duke of Normandy.

The battle was hard
And the men were ready to die.
William's archers were too good to beat.
Harold died with an arrow in his eye,
Harold died with an arrow in his eye.

William was conqueror.
You could say.
He went on to capture London
And was crowned on Christmas Day
And was crowned on Christmas Day.

Alasdair Stores (10)
Perse Preparatory School

Stage Fright On Friday (Freaky Friday)

I stood all alone on stage,
In front of the overwhelmed audience.
I was so petrified, I froze to stone.

My heart was racing rapidly,
Boom, boom, boom!
All of a sudden,
The lights flashed on
And suddenly blinded me.

I was saying to myself,
'Cool down'
and then I said to my brain,
'I'm an ice cube.'

Just then my manager whispered,
'It's time, time to start!'

Rachel Christie (10)
St John's Church Primary School, Peterborough

My Nightmare

I stepped onto the stage,
No sound could be heard.
My heart was beating, like a motorbike,
Full pelt.
All I could hear was
My heart beating as fast as it possibly
Could.

All of me was shaking with fear.
I wanted it to be over.
Flash!
As bright as lightning
Something blinded me!

Jemma Speight (10)
St John's Church Primary School, Peterborough

Witches' Poem
(In the style of Shakespeare)

Double, double, toil and trouble,
Fire burn and cauldron bubble.
Eye of wolf and toe of bear
Teeth of dog and skin of hare
Beak of duck and wing of bat
Tongue of snake and ear of cat
Go together like a newborn spell.
Listen to this, but never tell.
Double, double, toil and trouble,
Fire burn and cauldron bubble.

Double, double, toil and trouble,
Fire burn and cauldron bubble.
Fin of shark and baboon's bum
Mix it together, yum, yum, yum.
Tail of fox and nose of hog
Legs of spider and bark of log
Sugar and spice, mix it twice.
Claws of lion, squeak of mice.
Double, double, toil and trouble,
Fire burn and cauldron bubble.

Josh Munday & Emily Hammond (11)
St John's Church Primary School, Peterborough

Boo Who!

I stared like a predator looking at their prey.
My eyes were glued to the audience.
Suddenly,
Quick as a flash,
The light came on
And then I knew the long wait was over.
My heart started to slow down.
Boom! Boom! Boom!

Shayn Smith (11)
St John's Church Primary School, Peterborough

Witches' Poem

(In the style of Shakespeare)

Double, double, toil and trouble,
Fire burn and stomach turns.
Leg of fiddly drake,
In the cauldron bake.
Double, double, toil and trouble,
Fire burn and stomach turns.
Leg of frog,
Hair of dog.
Double, double, toil and trouble,
Fire burn and stomach turns.
Tail of dragon, eye of pigs,
Boil it up with lots of figs.
Double, double, toil and trouble,
Fire burn and stomach turns.

Nathan Brown (11)
St John's Church Primary School, Peterborough

Frightful

Walking worriedly onto the stage
Boom! Boom!
Went my heart.
Nothing but darkness,
Silent darkness!
Whoosh!
The lights, blinding,
Blinding like the sun.

'Alas poor Yorrick, I knew him well.'

Joanna Pullinger (11)
St John's Church Primary School, Peterborough

Afraid Of The Dark?

It was nerve-wracking
As I stepped on stage.
Darkness!
The closer I got to the middle of the stage,
The more I felt like I was going to be sick.
Then . . .
Bang!
The darkness disappeared,
The flickering light was blinding me.

Even though I was frightened,
I felt less sick.
I don't know why, but
Suddenly,
I felt quite good,
I felt like a millionaire!
It was *cool.*

Andrew Stephenson (10)
St John's Church Primary School, Peterborough

Stage Fright

Racing, rivers rushing
Like blood around my heart.
The closer it came,
The more I panicked.
As I stepped on stage,
Cheering, clapping.
My heart kept pounding,
Beating like a drum.
But all I saw was
Darkness.
Darkness!

Stephen Burn (11)
St John's Church Primary School, Peterborough

Witches' Poem
(In the style of Shakespeare)

Double, double, toil and trouble
Fire burn and cauldron bubble
Whisker of a silky cat
Boiling in the witches' vat
Tongue of rat and heart of monkey
Eye of skunk and ear of donkey
Howl of wolf and cry of lark
Roar of bear and stray dog's bark
Double, double, toil and trouble
Fire burn and cauldron bubble!

Emma Hume (11)
St John's Church Primary School, Peterborough

Stage Poem

I was slipping, sliding
Along the browny, blacky stage.
I was scared.
Bang!
The lights came on . . .

It's time for my part now.

Marina Hansen (10)
St John's Church Primary School, Peterborough

My Scary Stage Fright

As I stepped onto the gigantic stage,
The colourful lights
Flickered.
What was that?
It was nearly time
To start the show.

Lynette Barnett (11)
St John's Church Primary School, Peterborough

Stage Of Darkness

Slowly, silently,
I came closer towards the darkness,
Nothing but darkness.
Flash!
The lights flashed before my very eyes . . .

It's time to start.

Stuart Firth (11)
St John's Church Primary School, Peterborough

What Is Fog?

Fog is a giant's breath
Floating in the air.

Fog is a grey cover
Covering the air.

Fog is a forest of greyhounds
Striding.

Fog is a stone
All grey and beautiful.

Connor Wormald (9)
Swaffham Bulbeck Primary School

Cobra - Haiku

Still on forest floor
Gazing at the shining sun
Bathing in its shade.

Matty Garner (9)
Swaffham Bulbeck Primary School

Morning Sounds

Car engines roaring to start
Mum's alarm clock bleeping
The toaster popping
Lunch boxes crashing
Kettles whistling
Dogs barking
Letter boxes clattering
Dad munching his biscuits.

Adam Judge (9)
Swaffham Bulbeck Primary School

Pony - Haiku

Ponies are playful
Quiet in the grassy field
Munching on carrots.

Shannon Wright (8)
Swaffham Bulbeck Primary School

Wolf - Haiku

Behind a grey hill
Hiding from other mean wolves
Still as a statue.

Ben Barrett (9)
Swaffham Bulbeck Primary School

Cheetah - Haiku

Trying to find prey
Wind blowing my fluffy fur
Moonlight shining bright.

Megan Pedersen (9)
Swaffham Bulbeck Primary School

What Is A Cloud?

A cloud is white fluff
On a light blue piece of paper.

A cloud is pink candyfloss
On blue paint.

A cloud is cotton wool
On a blue-coloured sheet.

A cloud is a giant marshmallow
Floating in the air.

A cloud is soft wool
Floating away in the sky.

Sam King (8)
Swaffham Bulbeck Primary School

What Are Clouds Like?

The clouds are like foggy smoke
Coming out of a chimney.

The clouds are like white, fluffy shapes
On a blue piece of paper.

The clouds are like soft, woolly carpets
Floating in the sky.

The clouds are like pieces of cotton wool
Floating in the heavens.

The clouds are like pieces of white paper
Up above in the sky.

Poppy Crossley (8)
Swaffham Bulbeck Primary School

Similes

As soft as snow
As rough as a dog's paw
As gentle as a bear
As sharp as a knife
As ugly as an octopus
As bad-tempered as a bear
As beautiful as a queen
As cold as snow
As hot as the sun
As peaceful as a dolphin
As white as snow
As brave as a tiger
As graceful as a rabbit
As quiet as a panda.

Hannalise Tirrell (7)
Swaffham Bulbeck Primary School

What Are Snowflakes?

They are like miniature footballs
Being kicked from the sky.

Snowflakes are like tissues
Cut up into white flakes.

White snowflakes are like little pieces of paper
On the floor.

Chelsea Oliver (8)
Swaffham Bulbeck Primary School

What Is A Star?

A star is like a little light shining from the sky.
A star is a piece of yellow tissue paper raining from the sky.
A star is like silver, glittery paper stuck on the sky.

Ellie Crossley (8)
Swaffham Bulbeck Primary School

Haikus

Parrot
In the tree I sit
Slowly pecking at my fruit
I feel very safe.

Gecko
Pouncing on a moth
Diving into a small crack
To eat it alone.

Butterfly
Landing on flowers
Then flying ever onwards
To the next flower.

Amy Mockridge (7)
Swaffham Bulbeck Primary School

What Is Rain?

The rain is little drops of water
That falls out of a bubbly cloud.
The rain is big tears
Falling to the ground.
The rain comes down
As quick as scampering mice.
The rain is shiny diamonds
Floating to the ground.

Shannon Manchett (9)
Swaffham Bulbeck Primary School

The Moon

The moon looks like cheese with a big bit out of it.
The moon is like a giant mouth smiling.
The moon is like a massive piece of yellow sponge cake.
The moon is a car's wheel.

Dominic Ambrose (9)
Swaffham Bulbeck Primary School

What Is The Rain?

The rain is like pieces of gold
Falling from the sky.

The rain is like golden jewels
Floating down from Heaven.

The rain is like pieces of broken glass
Drifting down from Heaven.

The rain is like glitter
Falling from a big, blue cushion.

The rain is like little fairies
Flying down from the clouds.

The rain is like pieces of sponge
Slowly floating down.

Laura Foreman (8)
Swaffham Bulbeck Primary School

The Clouds

The clouds are fluffy sheep
Leaping in the sky.

The clouds are woolly jumpers
All cosy and warm.

The clouds are balls of fluff
That kittens love to play with.

The clouds are pieces of cotton wool
That you use to dab your eye.

The clouds are big, white balloons
Floating in the sky.

The clouds are huge, grey water bombs
Ready to burst.

Ellen Rayner (8)
Swaffham Bulbeck Primary School

Rivers

Bubbling gently, quietly,
Minnows swimming with the current,
Still as a statue, the heron waits.
The river gets bigger, sparkling in the sun,
The river's still getting bigger,
The current's getting faster,
The river's getting sandy,
Suddenly the river makes an amazing dive,
Splash!
It's the bottom of a waterfall,
The river's turned into a lake . . .
Darting minnows, big pike,
Swallows skim the water,
An osprey dives . . .

Joe Acklam (10)
Swaffham Bulbeck Primary School

The Journey Down The River

Down the R
                I
                    V
                        E
                            R I go
Round the meander I flow
I see a turquoise kingfisher fly over me
I see a heron dive into me to eat some fish
I'm getting bigger and bigger in the river
Suddenly I'm in the sea.

Hannah Hudson (10)
Swaffham Bulbeck Primary School

The Journey Of A River

I start off at the top of a mountain,
Bubbling as I trickle down a slope.
Darting minnows swimming around me,
Under a bridge I go, sparkling.
I am getting wider, turning into a river,
A beautiful, turquoise kingfisher flies over me,
A boat is on me with laughing children on board.
I go past a field with chestnut horses munching grass,
Willow tree branches dangle into me.
I am getting bigger still,
A heron is catching fish,
There is sand around me,
I am the sea.

Jessica Rayner (10)
Swaffham Bulbeck Primary School

Winter Birds

In a cold, white wintery garden,
Lived a fluffy barn owl
With black, shiny eyes.
He stood on the pond,
Covered with ice.
In the black, night sky,
He swooped up
And landed on the window sill,
Scraping at the glass,
Trying to get into the warm.

Emily Rawlinson (10)
Swaffham Bulbeck Primary School

Up In The Mountain

Up in the mountain, the river splashes against borders
And rushes down   W
                    A
                    T
                    E
                    R   falls and goes into a bigger river.
It is going under a bridge.
It is going slower now, it is at the mouth of the sea.
Here we go, into the wavy sea.

Jake Cronin (10)
Swaffham Bulbeck Primary School

Apples

Dotty and round,
A soft, crunching sound,
As red as a rose,
The apple soon goes,
The apple's so juicy,
The smell's so fruity,
An apple for lunch,
Crunch! Crunch! Crunch!

Molly Preston (10)
Swaffham Bulbeck Primary School

Winter Birds - Haikus

Penguin
Waddling towards pools,
Catching fish as it walks by,
Black and white hunter.

Goose
Stumble, stagger, *bang!*
Swims slowly, fears the hunter,
Brother of the swan.

Martin Lively (10)
Swaffham Bulbeck Primary School

What's The Point In Life?

What's the point in life?
All we do is walk and talk and eat.
There's nothing we do that's really important.
We work for money, but why?
We make friends, fall in love,
We have relations, family,
We go to school, get an education,
For no reason at all.
We live, do things that don't matter,
Then die!

Sabrina Taylor (10)
Swaffham Bulbeck Primary School

Swooping Heron

Swooping heron standing there
In the icy cold water,
Waiting for a fish to come.
The tall, thin, freezing cold heron,
It's got a long beak and lovely green eyes,
A black rippling feather grows from its head.
Suddenly he sees a ripple and a splash in the water.
He ducks his head under the water and the fish has gone.

Aaron Smith (10)
Swaffham Bulbeck Primary School

Penguin

Waddling slowly through the ice and snow,
Clambering up on an iceberg flapping his wings,
Trying to fly, then *smack!* on the floor.
Plunging into the ice-cold, Arctic water he goes,
Swimming to the surface,
Fish clutched tightly in his beak,
Tipping squirming fish down his throat.
Snow falling on his fat belly,
His eyes darting,
Making sure there's no polar bear in sight . . .
Diving into the sea once more.

Alex Garner (10)
Swaffham Bulbeck Primary School

A River's Day

Ducks quacking on the water top,
Into the brook with a calming *plop!*
Over the edge, down the fall,
Into the lake, making a pool.
Fish jumping over and out,
With children standing by
With a shout, shout, shout!
Into the sea I make my way
And I'm very tired by the end of the day.

Miriam Willmott (11)
Swaffham Bulbeck Primary School

Leaves

Leaves are swirling and twirling,
Some are red and some are brown,
The autumn leaves are falling,
Rustling all the way down.

Crunching underneath your feet,
Across the forest floor,
There is so much colour,
I just can't wait for some more.

Tilly Newbury (11)
Swaffham Bulbeck Primary School

Winter Birds - Haikus

Penguin
Waddling on the ice
On the freezing cold, big lake
Falls on his belly.

Owl
Silently gliding
Swooping down towards its prey
The mouse is dead.

Zoe Ball (10)
Swaffham Bulbeck Primary School

Geese In Winter

Waddle, waddle, wild geese struggle,
Trying to keep their balance.
As the ice is melting,
The birds are calling across the winter lake.
The ice starts to crack in jagged lines.
Geese wobble as the surface splits.
The geese swoop off in the distant air,
Their huge wings beating gracefully and silently.

Lucy Parker (11)
Swaffham Bulbeck Primary School

Beyond The Door

(Based on 'The Door' by Miroslav Holub)

Go and open the door
Maybe outside there's
A water fountain pouring with water
Or a big pile of gold
Or a flying book.

Go and open the door
Maybe there are lots of spiders and bats
Maybe a pot of gold
Or some birds singing
Or hens running around.

Go and open the door
If there's a magic tree
There will be a magic bird.

Amy Mills (8)
Teversham CE Primary School

Beyond The Door

(Based on 'The Door' by Miroslav Holub)

Go and open the door
Maybe outside
There's a water fountain
Or a wishing well
Or a pile of gold.

Go and open the door
Maybe there's a magic tree
Maybe there's a magic tree house
Or a magic spell book
Or Disneyland.

Go and open the door
If there's a poisonous snake
It will get scared away.

Katie Logan (7)
Teversham CE Primary School

Beyond The Door

(Based on 'The Door' by Miroslav Holub)

Go and open the door
Maybe outside there's
A magic tree house
A magic spell book
Or a magic tree.

Go and open the door
Maybe there's a sandy beach
Maybe there's a sunny sky
Or children making sandcastles
Or having a swim in the sea.

Go and open the door
If there's another door
It will open.

Jessica Adams (8)
Teversham CE Primary School

Beyond The Door

(Based on 'The Door' by Miroslav Holub)

Go and open the door
Maybe outside there's
A pile of gold
A garden of red flowers
Or a pond of green frogs.

Go and open the door
Maybe there's a golden leaf
Maybe a waterfall
Or a city of birds and trees
Or red-hot sand.

Go and open the door
If you do
It will lead to another door.

Scarlett Diver (7)
Teversham CE Primary School

The Sound Of Music

When I walk in the flower fields,
When I skip in the grass,
I feel a feeling of happiness, a feeling of love.
My brain feels the rhythm, my heart feels the beat
And I feel the sound of music.
When I smell the purple lavender,
When I sit by the blue sea,
I feel a feeling of happiness, a feeling of love.
My brain feels the rhythm, my heart feels the beat
And I feel the sound of music.
When I climb up green hills,
When I paddle through sweet streams,
I feel a feeling of happiness, a feeling of love.
My brain feels the rhythm, my heart feels the beat
And I feel the sound of music.
I sing with my heart
And watch it go to the sky.
I jump up and down with a great feeling of joy.
I look at my city,
The beautiful city of Cambridge,
I feel that feeling all over myself,
That feeling of happiness, that feeling of love,
My brain feels the rhythm, my heart feels the beat,
Oh, the wonderful sound of music.

Rama Lakshman (8)
Teversham CE Primary School

Lions

Lions are big, lions are scary,
Lions are very, very hairy.
Lions have big teeth,
Lions have extremely loud roars,
Lions have very sharp claws.

Ashley Reid (8)
Teversham CE Primary School

Ten Little Cats

Ten little cats playing on a washing line,
One fell off, then there were nine.
Nine little cats were at a fête,
One thought the music was too loud and then there were eight.
Eight little cats thinking about Heaven,
One got bored, then there were seven.
Seven little cats playing with sticks,
One tripped over, then there were six.
Six little cats going for a dive,
One remembered he was scared, then there were five.
Five little cats putting on a tour,
One got embarrassed, then there were four.
Four little cats climbing up a tree,
One fell down, then there were three.
Three little cats playing a new game,
One got tired, then there were two.
Two little cats sunbathing in the sun,
One got too hot, then there was one.
One little cat getting everything done,
He went off, then there was none.

Laura Shephard (8)
Teversham CE Primary School

When I Met An Alien

I went to see an alien in space
And it had a terrible face.
It was covered in spots
That were completely round dots
And each had its own perfect place.

Jake Brown (8)
Teversham CE Primary School

What If There's An Elephant?

What if there's a pink elephant?
What if there's a blue elephant?
What if there's a flying elephant?
What if there's a tap dancing elephant?
What if there's a tightrope walking elephant?
What if there's a Britney Spears elephant?
What if there's a gymnast elephant?
What if there's a know-it-all elephant?
What if there's a show-off elephant?
What if there's a millionaire elephant?
What if there's a triangular elephant?
What if there's a rectangular elephant?
What if there's an evil elephant?
What if there's a drowning elephant?
What if there's a bungee-jumping elephant?
What if there's a jockey elephant?
What if there's a ballet dancing elephant?
What if there's a Harry Potter elephant?
What if there's a skinny elephant?
What if there's an angel elephant?
What if there's a tiny elephant?
Well, there won't be a tiny elephant!

Melissa Pettitt (8)
Teversham CE Primary School

Beyond The Door

(Based on 'The Door' by Miroslav Holub)

Go and open the door,
Maybe outside there's a sea full of dolphins,
A big pot of gold or a tree house,
Go and open the door,
Maybe there are some monkeys,
Maybe a bunch of men or some girls or a tree,
Go and open the door if there is another door,
It will take you to another world.

Abigail Bell (8)
Teversham CE Primary School

Once I Met An Alien

Once I met an alien
Who came straight down to Earth,
But he had been up in space
Ever since his birth.
But then one day he went away
In his little ship,
Everything had gone with him
Except a little computer chip.

Jake Bowden (8)
Teversham CE Primary School

In My Brand New Clothes

I went to the seaside,
In my brand new clothes,
Went to the rock pools
And the rocks were shining, shining.

I went to the seaside,
In my brand new clothes,
Looked in the sky
And saw the sun was shining, shining.

I went to the seaside,
In my brand new clothes,
Saw the sand, sprinkled the sparkling sand,
The sand was shining, shining.

Olivia Brown (7)
William Hildyard CE Primary School

Christmas

S anta Claus
A t morning sleeping
N ight away on his sleigh
T eaching children to be good
A nd elves making mummy mugs

C hristmas is coming
L et's be quiet as Santa's coming to town
A nd be asleep and don't make a sound
U se the baubles to hang on the tree
S anta Claus is coming to town.

Katie Webb (8)
William Hildyard CE Primary School

The Extraordinary Ship

The extraordinary ship
It holds 100,000 passengers
Huge, strong, elegant
Like a whale in the sea
Like a car in a race
It makes me feel slow
Like a snail hardly moving
The extraordinary ship
It reminds us how strong we are.

Daniel E Luff (10)
William Hildyard CE Primary School

The Empty Beach

The empty beach
Golden sands
Huge, lonely, calming
Like a white room with no exit
Like a place where only you exist
It makes me feel alone
I feel like I'm the only one on Earth
The empty beach.
Reminds us how company counts.

Ben Winspear (11)
William Hildyard CE Primary School

The Hyper Donkey

The hyper donkey
He is very old
Is fat, ugly and short
He is wider than a rhino
He has got more energy than a monkey
He makes me feel extremely tired
Like a tired out camel
The hyper donkey
The hyper donkey makes me think of me.

Oliver Lansell (11)
William Hildyard CE Primary School

The Fluffy Cloud

The fluffy cloud
It is full of water.
Wet, white, dripping
Like a sheep with no head or legs.
Like candyfloss all light and airy
It makes me feel fluffy and warm.
Like a fluffy thing that people want to eat.
The fluffy cloud
Reminds me of the water cycle to help us stay alive.

Thomas Burton (10)
William Hildyard CE Primary School

Space

I always dream about travelling in space,
It would be so wonderful to gaze
At stars and planets twinkling like crystal and gold,
Comets speeding by fast and bold.

Our Milky Way has this and more,
This glittering galaxy I want to explore,
Then on to the other galaxies I will fly,
More and more wonders I will spy.

Hasnain Datoo (11)
William Hildyard CE Primary School

The Mighty Lancaster

The mighty Lancaster
Made to destroy the dams.
Elegant, withstanding, ear-splitting,
It was the terror of the sky.
Like the modern jet today.
It makes me feel about a small finger's height tall
As I stand under its bulk.
The mighty Lancaster
Makes me think of the pilots
That lost their lives in the Lancaster
As it flies away.

Ben Windsor (11)
William Hildyard CE Primary School

The Golden Beach

The golden beach,
Made from ground up rocks.
Soft, yellow, sandy,
Like the colour of the sun,
Like trickling water beneath our feet.
It makes me want to dig a hole
As deep as the sea beside the beach.
The golden beach,
It reminds me of my holidays.

William Burton (10)
William Hildyard CE Primary School

Sports Day

Sports day is full of embarrassment
I tried to win the race but I couldn't
All the awful moments I know
But I hate the words ready, steady, go!
We can have a good time as well
But I am rubbish at throwing
It's a horrible day and hard
But home is the best of all
It would be even nicer
If we had a swimming pool!

Rebecca Potton (8)
William Hildyard CE Primary School

All About Dragons!

D is for dancing which the dragon likes.
R is for rubbish, a dragon's meal.
A is for ambulance. You may need it if he sees you.
G is for God who made us.
O is for others who we like and that includes the dragon.
N is for noise, which we like to make.
S is for sad to let this poem end.

Marcus Cook (8)
William Hildyard CE Primary School

Shells

Shells you see and hear the sea,
Hear the sea and the lovely breeze.
Shells on your ear, you hear, you hear.
Lovely ice cream you eat at the beach.
Lovely fish you see, you see.
The sea, you hear its crashing on the rocks.

Charlotte Hussey (7)
William Hildyard CE Primary School

The Thin Cat

The thin cat
Is like a thin pencil
Playful, tiring, active
Like a ball that never stops bouncing
Like a head that never stops purring
It makes me feel tired
I feel like a very tall person
The thin cat
Reminds how animals are so important.

Danielle Raven (10)
William Hildyard CE Primary School

At The Seaside

The wonderful sparkling sand,
The waving, thundering sea,
The crunching rocks about,
The wonderful sea creatures in the rock pool,
Taste the creamy ice creams with flakes on top,
Playing cricket on the beach,
Whacking the ball for another six,
The beach, the beach,
What a wonderful place to be.

Jake Brown (7)
William Hildyard CE Primary School

The Seaside

Put a seashell upon your ear
You can hear the sea
Hear the sea
Hear the sea
When I go to the sea
I can smell the sea
Smell the sea
Smell the sea
When I swim in the sea I can
Taste the sea
Taste the sea
Taste the sea.

Laura Aldington (7)
William Hildyard CE Primary School

Seaside Things

The fishes are swimming,
The people are laughing,
The boats are sailing
And the seaweed is swaying.
The shells are shining,
The sand twinkles like the sun,
The sea is glowing,
The sun is shining
And everybody's having fun!

Leah Potton (7)
William Hildyard CE Primary School

Sea Creatures

One and a half litres of water
One ton of seaweed
Two litres of whales
One and a half miles of dolphins
400 litres of jellyfish
Six and a half tons of crabs
The whole sea full of starfish
A kettle full of fishes
A classroom full of rocks
A boxful of sharks
A flat full of swordfishes
A school full of shells
A book full of sea horses
Now when all these ingredients melt into one
You'll find the sea I wrote about in this poem.

Sharnee Baker (11)
Woodston Primary School

Goodbye Mummy

It's sad for us to see you go,
The Greenline bus for home.
You hug us and you shed a tear,
'I will be back for Christmas, dear.'

Oh dear Mummy, we love you so,
It's such a shame you have to go.
We do not want to see you depart,
So we will have to smother you with jam tarts.

Jordan Greer (11)
Woodston Primary School

The Monster Under My Bed

I told my mum one day, 'There's a monster under my bed,'
She told me not to be so scared.
I don't know if it's a monster with no head,
Or a monster who has a smell that can't be bear-ed.
I know there's a monster under my bed.

Sometimes I see its scary shadow appear on the ground,
I feel its hairy ears,
Sometimes I even hear its screeching sound.
This monster's one of my greatest fears,
I know there's a monster under my bed.

One day I was very brave,
I looked under the bed.
There was nothing but a bundle of clothes in the shape of a cave,
The shadow was only my ted.
I know there's not a monster under my bed!

Hannah Hillan (11)
Woodston Primary School

Football Fantasy

F ootball is fantastic
O h, it is a great game
O h, it is a sight
T he crowd are screaming
B ut it's energy-taking
A ll the players playing
L ots of points for the teams, at
L ast the game ended!

Jamie Cook (11)
Woodston Primary School

The Stages In A Womb For A Baby

I was created in my mother's womb,
In a dark, pink sack I settled in,
Listening to a heart that never stops beating.
First I am an embryo,
Secondly a foetus,
Then I am a little thing you call a baby.
After 26 weeks of my mother's pregnancy,
My eyes are being formed
And my heart is starting to beat.
Now I can see,
Kicking and turning, I move.
Then the next thing you know,
I am born.
Out into the dangerous world I leapt,
Helpless, naked, crying aloud.
Finally my mother can rest,
As I suck upon her breast.

Amy McLennan (11)
Woodston Primary School

The Sun

I am a star
That lights up the sky.
I give heat to people.
I look over the Earth,
The Earth orbits around me.
I am the hottest star
In the universe and galaxy.

Justin Butler (11)
Woodston Primary School

Shadows

I have a big shadow that goes in and out of me
And what he is there for, no reason can I see.
He is very much like me from head to toe,
I've named him Friendly Joe.
The weirdest thing about him is that he likes to grow,
Not like us children, who grow extremely slow,
For sometimes he shoots up taller than an Indian rubber ball
And sometimes he gets so little that there's hardly any of him at all.

My shadow is strange,
Well what can you say?
It's plain and boring, simply all day the same.

Michaela Coley (11)
Woodston Primary School

Night Falls

Night falls with a sleepy head,
Night falls when you're in your bed.

Night falls with stars and the moon,
Night falls, then morning.

Night falls when bats fly,
Night falls with a sleepy eye.

Night falls with a kiss from your brother,
Night falls with the love of your mother,
Tucking you up in bed.

Jade Wheeler (11)
Woodston Primary School

Recipe For A Friend

First take a sprinkle of kindness,
A lump of trust,
A sack of friendship,
A spoon of funniness,
A kilo of love,
An ounce of beauty,
A nip of fun,
Three bags of strength,
A cup of cuddles,
A centimetre of sensitivity.

Get all these together
And bake them in the oven for an hour.
Take it out of the oven
And there will be your best friend.
Hopefully you'll stay together forever!

Charlotte Stephenson (11)
Woodston Primary School

My Race

I was at the starting line waiting to go,
The sun was blazing down upon me.
I got hotter by the second.
I was waiting for the horn to sound.
It went, I ran,
I stumbled, I tripped.
I got to my feet and hoped not to be last.

Richard Thomas (11)
Woodston Primary School